OPPOSING
VIEWPOINTS®
SERIES

D0001100

America's Changing Demographics

Other Books of Related Interest

Opposing Viewpoints Series

Human Migration
Identity Politics
Privilege in America
Uber, Lyft, Airbnb, and the Sharing Economy
The Wealth Gap

At Issue Series

Gender Politics
Gerrymandering and Voting Districts
Male Privilege
Populism in the Digital Age
Reproductive Rights

Current Controversies Series

Antifa and the Radical Left
Are There Two Americas?
Deporting Immigrants
LGBTQ Rights
The Two-Party System in the United States

> # "Congress shall make no law … abridging the freedom of speech, or of the press."

First Amendment to the US Constitution

The basic foundation of our democracy is the First Amendment guarantee of freedom of expression. The Opposing Viewpoints series is dedicated to the concept of this basic freedom and the idea that it is more important to practice it than to enshrine it.

**OPPOSING
VIEWPOINTS®
SERIES**

America's Changing Demographics

Martin Gitlin, Book Editor

GREENHAVEN
PUBLISHING

Published in 2020 by Greenhaven Publishing, LLC
353 3rd Avenue, Suite 255, New York, NY 10010

First Edition

Articles in Greenhaven Publishing anthologies are often edited for length to meet page
requirements. In addition, original titles of these works are changed to clearly present
the main thesis and to explicitly indicate the author's opinion. Every effort is made to
ensure that Greenhaven Publishing accurately reflects the original intent of the authors.
Every effort has been made to trace the owners of the copyrighted material.

Cover image: elenabsl/Shutterstock.com

Library of Congress Cataloging-in-Publication Data

Names: Gitlin, Marty, author.
Title: America's changing demographics / Martin Gitlin.
Description: First Edition. | New York : Greenhaven Publishing, 2020. |
  Includes bibliographical references and index. | Audience: Grade 9 to
  12.
Identifiers: LCCN 2019020303| ISBN 9781534506015 (library binding) | ISBN
  9781534506008 (paperback)
Subjects: LCSH: United States—Population—Juvenile literature. |
  Population forecasting—United States—Juvenile literature. | Baby boom
  generation—United States—Juvenile literature. | Immigrants—United
  States—Juvenile literature.
Classification: LCC HB3505 .G58 2019 | DDC 304.60973—dc23
LC record available at https://lccn.loc.gov/2019020303

Manufactured in the United States of America

Website: http://greenhavenpublishing.com

Contents

Chapter 3: Does a Growing Population Create a Growing Problem?

Chapter 4: What Is America's Electoral Future?

The Importance of Opposing Viewpoints

Perhaps every generation experiences a period in time in which the populace seems especially polarized, starkly divided on the important issues of the day and gravitating toward the far ends of the political spectrum and away from a consensus-facilitating middle ground. The world that today's students are growing up in and that they will soon enter into as active and engaged citizens is deeply fragmented in just this way. Issues relating to terrorism, immigration, women's rights, minority rights, race relations, health care, taxation, wealth and poverty, the environment, policing, military intervention, the proper role of government—in some ways, perennial issues that are freshly and uniquely urgent and vital with each new generation—are currently roiling the world.

If we are to foster a knowledgeable, responsible, active, and engaged citizenry among today's youth, we must provide them with the intellectual, interpretive, and critical-thinking tools and experience necessary to make sense of the world around them and of the all-important debates and arguments that inform it. After all, the outcome of these debates will in large measure determine the future course, prospects, and outcomes of the world and its peoples, particularly its youth. If they are to become successful members of society and productive and informed citizens, students need to learn how to evaluate the strengths and weaknesses of someone else's arguments, how to sift fact from opinion and fallacy, and how to test the relative merits and validity of their own opinions against the known facts and the best possible available information. The landmark series Opposing Viewpoints has been providing students with just such critical-thinking skills and exposure to the debates surrounding society's most urgent contemporary issues for many years, and it continues to serve this essential role with undiminished commitment, care, and rigor.

The key to the series's success in achieving its goal of sharpening students' critical-thinking and analytic skills resides in its title—

Opposing Viewpoints. In every intriguing, compelling, and engaging volume of this series, readers are presented with the widest possible spectrum of distinct viewpoints, expert opinions, and informed argumentation and commentary, supplied by some of today's leading academics, thinkers, analysts, politicians, policy makers, economists, activists, change agents, and advocates. Every opinion and argument anthologized here is presented objectively and accorded respect. There is no editorializing in any introductory text or in the arrangement and order of the pieces. No piece is included as a "straw man," an easy ideological target for cheap point-scoring. As wide and inclusive a range of viewpoints as possible is offered, with no privileging of one particular political ideology or cultural perspective over another. It is left to each individual reader to evaluate the relative merits of each argument— as he or she sees it, and with the use of ever-growing critical-thinking skills—and grapple with his or her own assumptions, beliefs, and perspectives to determine how convincing or successful any given argument is and how the reader's own stance on the issue may be modified or altered in response to it.

This process is facilitated and supported by volume, chapter, and selection introductions that provide readers with the essential context they need to begin engaging with the spotlighted issues, with the debates surrounding them, and with their own perhaps shifting or nascent opinions on them. In addition, guided reading and discussion questions encourage readers to determine the authors' point of view and purpose, interrogate and analyze the various arguments and their rhetoric and structure, evaluate the arguments' strengths and weaknesses, test their claims against available facts and evidence, judge the validity of the reasoning, and bring into clearer, sharper focus the reader's own beliefs and conclusions and how they may differ from or align with those in the collection or those of their classmates.

Research has shown that reading comprehension skills improve dramatically when students are provided with compelling, intriguing, and relevant "discussable" texts. The subject matter of these collections could not be more compelling, intriguing, or urgently relevant to today's students and the world they are poised to inherit. The anthologized articles and the reading and discussion questions that are included with them also provide the basis for stimulating, lively, and passionate classroom debates. Students who are compelled to anticipate objections to their own argument and identify the flaws in those of an opponent read more carefully, think more critically, and steep themselves in relevant context, facts, and information more thoroughly. In short, using discussable text of the kind provided by every single volume in the Opposing Viewpoints series encourages close reading, facilitates reading comprehension, fosters research, strengthens critical thinking, and greatly enlivens and energizes classroom discussion and participation. The entire learning process is deepened, extended, and strengthened.

For all of these reasons, Opposing Viewpoints continues to be exactly the right resource at exactly the right time—when we most need to provide readers with the critical-thinking tools and skills that will not only serve them well in school but also in their careers and their daily lives as decision-making family members, community members, and citizens. This series encourages respectful engagement with and analysis of opposing viewpoints and fosters a resulting increase in the strength and rigor of one's own opinions and stances. As such, it helps make readers "future ready," and that readiness will pay rich dividends for the readers themselves, for the citizenry, for our society, and for the world at large.

Introduction

> "*Change of this magnitude acts
> on us psychologically, not just
> electorally. It is the crucial context
> uniting the core political conflicts
> of this era—Obama and Trump's
> presidencies, the rise of reactionary
> new social movements and thinkers,
> the wars over political correctness
> on campuses and representation in
> Hollywood, the power of #MeToo
> and BlackLivesMatter, the fights over
> immigration.*"
>
> —*Ezra Klein*[1]

Americans are changing. If a person who lived a century ago was brought back to walk the sidewalks of an American town or city today, they would notice quite a difference in the people who walked among them. The largely white, European-descended citizens they were used to seeing in the last century likely have been replaced by a greater number of Hispanics, Asian Americans, African Americans, and people of Middle Eastern backgrounds. The white population that for so long was considered "all American" is aging and has a low birth rate. The minority population is comparatively much younger.

The shift in demographics that seems destined to continue well into the twenty-first century is not in itself a problem. But most believe that how the American people and its institutions react to it certainly can prove troublesome if those changes are not accepted and the nation does not effectively adapt. The level of success in adjusting to the aging of baby boomers and the growth of the minority population will go a long way in determining the future of the United States.

The issue of immigration has already caused great consternation. The promise and push of President Donald Trump to build a wall along the border of the United States and Mexico has received support from those who believe his claims that Hispanic immigrants steal jobs while bringing drugs and criminality into the country. Those that rail against Trump's assertions state he is simply a racist who has indicated that he would welcome immigrants from nations with dominant white populations.

Experts believe that the moral debates that revolve around demographic changes in America must end in a consensus before pragmatic solutions to resulting issues can be effectively tackled. Among those issues is health care. Millions of baby boomers born after World War II as one of the largest generations in United States history are retiring and aging. Who will take their place in the workforce? How well will the health care system provide for them? Can the liberal call for Medicare for All create a cost-effective structure that satisfies boomers and their offspring?

Much will depend on the political climate, which in itself reflects demographic shifts. Many feel the 2016 presidential campaign that placed Trump in the White House and the 2018 midterms that were viewed as a backlash against his policies were both indicative of such population changes. It has been stated that the surprising 2016 election was the last gasp of aging, conservative white Americans, who streamed to the polls and voted heavily in favor of Trump. It has also been claimed that the midterms two years later that resulted in a Democratic takeover of the House and a record number of women and comparatively young representatives reflected a growing liberalism embraced by immigrants and youthful, more idealistic Americans.

Demographics will play a huge role in the political fight for the soul of America and determine the fate of the country regarding a wide range of issues such as gun violence, LGBTQ rights, climate change, income inequality, health management, abortion, immigration, and the costs and accessibility of a college education. It has been claimed that people grow more conservative as they age. Republicans certainly hope that is true as polls have shown a distinct liberal leaning among young Americans and immigrants. The popularity among many in the younger generations of such politicians as 2020 presidential candidate Beto O'Rourke and Democratic congresswoman Alexandria Ocasio-Cortez certainly indicates a swing to the political left.

The United States has been a melting pot since the late nineteenth century. The demographic changes it has experienced through immigration and the dying off of many in older, more conservative generations seems to promise more liberal slants on most issues unless the old adage about people growing more conservative with age proves accurate and changes the outlook. Many foresee a United States that is far more inclusive for racial and sexual minorities, active in the battle for gun control and against climate change, and energetic in its fight for fairness in taxation and income disparity.

Of more immediate attention is health care, which is both a moral and practical issue. Many youthful politicians that attract the support of younger Americans have promised to implement a Medicare for All system that provides what they claim can be affordable health care for all Americans. A demographic shift to a younger and perhaps more liberal society seems destined to play a role in the debate over the viability of Medicare for All. But the issue of how effectively and cost-efficiently the millions of aging baby boomers will be cared for as the mid-2000s approach must be debated and solved quickly. Many boomers have retired, and the oldest of that generation will reach the age of 75 by the year 2021.

A more youthful, diverse society promises vast changes to the future of America. The ability and willingness of Americans to distance themselves from the divisiveness that has marked the Trump era and work together to forge a positive path will go a long way in determining whether those changes will prove a success or failure. *Opposing Viewpoints: America's Changing Demographics* examines these issues and more in chapters titled "How Will Demographic Shifts Affect America's Political Landscape?" "How Will Its Aging Population Impact the United States?" "Does a Growing Population Create a Growing Problem?" and "What Is America's Electoral Future?" The demographic shifts in the United States cannot be avoided. What remains to be seen is how its citizens and its leaders react to them.

Notes

1. "White Threat in a Browning America," by Ezra Klein, Vox, July 30, 2018.

OPPOSING
VIEWPOINTS®
SERIES

CHAPTER 1

How Will Demographic Shifts Affect America's Political Landscape?

Chapter Preface

One cannot predict with certainty how the American youth of today will vote in the future. Such is impossible in a nation of diversity, one in which both youth and adults from distinctly different backgrounds embrace wildly divergent political views. Will future generations from rural communities and small towns grow more liberal than they have been traditionally? Will college students and city dwellers of the same age trend toward greater conservatism?

Only time will tell. But if the strength of current views on issues such as gun control, income inequality, climate change, and LGBTQ rights are any indication, the future of the United States could be one of strong inclusivity, airtight background checks on those seeking to purchase weapons, active US inclusion in the battle against global warming, and significantly higher taxes on the wealthy.

This chapter covers all those issues and seeks out potential trends in how demographic changes in the United States will affect them. Among those shifts are the graying and browning of America. Those representing the oldest generation, born before the baby boomers, mostly white and far more conservative than those who followed, are dying off. Boomers, many of whom maintained their conservative beliefs throughout their adult lives or skewed to the right after the 1960s, are also decreasing in numbers. Meanwhile, the increasing number of immigrants and the gaining of political power among those in younger generations indicate a more liberal society in the future.

One cannot predict how powerful national or world events will affect the political landscape. But even a cursory study of the demographic changes promised for the United States certainly indicates a shift to the left on a myriad of vexing and complicated issues that will continue to test the problem-solving abilities of Americans and their leaders.

> "*Young people across the US are doing what countless others have tried and failed to do: using grassroots strategies to take on the powerful gun lobby.*"

Young People Are Gunning for Gun Control

George Rennie

In the following viewpoint George Rennie offers a view from afar on gun control in the United States, expressed after yet another school shooting in 2018. Rennie argues that stronger gun laws can be achieved despite the efforts of the powerful National Rifle Association (NRA). The author's positivity is based to some degree on the strengthening of will and perceived political righteousness of students who have experienced gun violence and other young people fed up with the political inactivity among government leaders. Rennie cites such energy as a potential match in a power struggle against the NRA and gun rights lobbyists. George Rennie is a lecturer in American Politics and Lobbying Strategies at the University of Melbourne, Australia.

"Articulate US Teenagers Could Finally Force Action on Gun Control," by George Rennie, The Conversation, 03/15/2018. https://theconversation.com/articulate-us-teenagers-could-finally-force-action-on-gun-control-92272.

As you read, consider the following questions:

1. What view does the author express about the National Rifle Association?
2. Why is the author hopeful about the gun control issue?
3. Why does the author feel Congress has not acted on gun control since 1994?

On Wednesday in the US, thousands of students left their classrooms in a national day of action designed to force political change on gun crime. Following the recent shooting at Marjory Stoneman Douglas High School, this walkout is part of an extraordinary national movement. Young people across the US are doing what countless others have tried and failed to do: using grassroots strategies to take on the powerful gun lobby.

The US has an epidemic of gun crime. Mass shootings occur every day, and school shootings have become so common that over 170 schools and some 150,000 students have been affected by school-based gun violence since 1999.

Beyond the psychological trauma such attacks inflict, these shootings have a profound effect on academic success rates.

And yet, in spite of the overwhelming majority of Americans who want tighter gun control laws, very little is done to stem the presence of guns in schools, or the ability of Americans to access high-powered weaponry with relative ease.

Policy Inertia and the NRA

The main reason for this inertia is the extraordinary influence of the National Rifle Association (NRA). Since it turned to a more aggressive lobbying strategy in the 1970s, the NRA has helped redefine the meaning of the 2nd Amendment, bestowed a divine blessing on guns, and bent half of Congress to its will.

The NRA succeeds because it has created powerful (and mostly false or distorted) narratives to support gun use. It deploys familiar tropes to distract from tragedies. When gun-related tragedy hits, NRA-backed politicians call for "thoughts and prayers."

The reality of US gun deaths is set against such pro-gun arguments, and each tragedy widens the stark divide between those who associate guns with freedom, and those who see them as devices for terror. So, when others call for legislative action, as they did following the massacre at Sandy Hook and other mass shootings, the gun lobby scolds them for "politicising tragedy."

But murdered kids are political. Sandy Hook exposed the US to the faces of erstwhile happy kindergarteners, their lives snuffed out by a disturbed young man with easy access to guns. It's an all-too-familiar story for Americans and, by international comparison, a unique one at that.

Yet the resulting push for change soon turned to despair: many came to believe that if 26 deaths at an elementary school can't bring Congress to act, nothing can.

Gun Laws and the Possibility of Change

The last major piece of gun control legislation to pass Congress was the federal assault weapons ban in 1994. It was specifically designed to reduce the incidence of mass shootings, and targeted the enhanced killing power of assault rifles. But, under sustained attack from the gun lobby, the ban expired under its "sunset clause."

Since then, the one major piece of gun legislation in the US, in spite of the national rise in mass and school shootings, has been an act designed to protect gun manufacturers in 2005.

Now, for the first time in decades, there is a real possibility that some gun controls might be implemented. The NRA, as well as numerous politicians associated with it, are facing significant pressure to act.

Recent news footage showed Senator Marco Rubio and the NRA's Dana Loesh publicly sparring with students from Marjory Stoneman Douglas High, to a chorus of boos and jeers. Millions witnessed their discomfort.

This has already led to some action by states. Florida is looking to pass age restrictions and waiting periods for gun purchases, and Oregon has imposed gun prohibitions on domestic abusers and those with restraining orders.

Even President Donald Trump, who has been keen to show off his pro-gun credentials in the past, has recognised the public outcry. He has called for regulation of bump-stocks and age restrictions (though he is wavering on both).

The High School Advocates

The reason gun control looks possible right now is largely due to the students at Marjory Stoneman Douglas. Beyond the pressure they have been applying directly to the NRA and politicians, the students have been busy using advocating on social media, writing op-eds, organising rallies and walkouts, making media appearances, and pressuring companies to drop support for the NRA or pro-gun politicians.

As a result of these efforts, the students are presenting important, emotionally powerful counter-narratives to those of the gun lobby. They are offering examples of successful gun control and pointing out that guns in schools are the problem, not the solution. They are also forming a coalition in opposition to the well-organised 2-4 million members of the NRA and affiliated organisations.

Whether these efforts are successful or not will depend largely on whether they are sustained. This is why the gun lobby calls for "hopes and prayers" and to not "politicise tragedy." These are stalling tactics: if the NRA can wait it out, while at the same time applying pressure to its political allies, nothing gets done.

However, the gun lobby has not faced a political force like this before. While it is inevitable that media attention will eventually wane, the students from Marjory Stoneman Douglas and around the country have access to tools—such as social media—that circumvent traditional outlets. They also have the ability to draw the national spotlight back, especially via their use of rallies and walkouts.

These tactics reinvigorate the Democratic base and ratchet up the pressure on the Republicans, already jittery following a string of shock political losses.

If the passion and dedication they have shown so far is sustained, especially as the congressional midterm elections approach, the young people of the US might just be able do what no one has done in decades, and force action on gun control.

| "If guns are banned, lawful people, not criminals, will be denied a key method of using force—in defense of self and others."

Widespread Gun Ownership Increases Personal Safety

Sheldon Richman

In the following viewpoint Sheldon Richman argues that idealistic efforts to control gun violence are naïve and unrealistic. The author cites the ability for those yearning to buy guns to skirt potential background checks and purchase them illegally. The author also claims that many murders are avoided annually by those using guns as a means of self-defense. His arguments have been used often by gun rights advocates and have been statistically refuted by those who embrace the opposite side of the issue. Sheldon Richman is the former editor of The Freeman *and a contributor to* The Concise Encyclopedia of Economics. *He is the author of* Separating School and State: How to Liberate America's Families *and thousands of articles.*

As you read, consider the following questions:

1. What does the author believe is the "unseen" in the gun control debate?
2. What arguments does the author make in expressing his view that gun bans cannot work?
3. How does American economics enter the debate about gun control, according to the viewpoint?

The heinous shootings by young people at public schools around the country have predictably renewed calls for more gun control. Advocates of gun bans commit a classic fallacy that is usually associated with economic policy. But it fully applies to all government policy, including gun control.

In the nineteenth century, the French economist Frederic Bastiat explained that in order to understand the consequences of a policy, you must consider both "what is seen and what is unseen." This was also the "one lesson" taught by Bastiat's intellectual descendant, Henry Hazlitt, in his famous book *Economics in One Lesson*. Hazlitt identified the "persistent tendency of men to see only the immediate effects of a given policy, or its effects only on a special group, and to neglect to inquire what the long-run effects of that policy will be not only on that special group but on all groups. It is the fallacy of overlooking secondary consequences."

The famous case of neglecting the unseen, of course, is the broken shop window. Observers are likely to notice that a glass maker will have new income to spend. They miss that had the glass not been broken, the owner of the window could have spent his money to better his situation rather than merely to restore it. That's the unseen.

If you think this is a seldom-committed fallacy, just read the newspaper after the next hurricane or earthquake. Five'll get you ten that someone will herald the silver lining: reconstruction projects.

If we look at only obvious, primary consequences, we will badly misjudge circumstances and any resulting policy will be bad. That is one problem with gun control.

Unseen Gun Sales

Advocates of gun bans react to a shooting by saying that if the assailant had had no access to firearms, that shooting could not have occurred. Of course, that is true: the shooting required a gun. But this proves much less than the controllers think. It doesn't mean that had the killer not been able to get a gun legally, he couldn't have gotten one at all. Fans of the Brady law, which requires a waiting period and background check for gun buyers, rejoice that tens of thousands of people have had gun applications turned down. (Most were not violent criminals.) But that's not the end of the story. Will a thug who is turned away from a gun shop give up so easily? Or is he apt to go into the black market to buy a firearm? Worse, might he not break into a gun shop or someone's home to steal a gun?

Gun control runs aground on this simple fact: people who would use guns to break laws would also break laws to use guns.

The controllers see the turn-down at the gun counter. They don't see, and therefore they don't take account of, the alternative methods of acquiring firearms.

Unseen Victims

The failure to look for the unseen does not stop there. After each mass shooting, we hear recited the statistics on how many people are murdered by gunshot each year. The implication is that without guns, the total murder rate would be reduced by that number. We are also reminded of how many accidental shootings occur (the firearms accident rate, however, has been falling), and are led to believe that if legal gun possession were severely restricted, fewer people would die each year from gunshots. Not true.

To be sure, some people who were killed might be alive today. But some who were not killed might have been. How so? It might come as a surprise, because it gets no publicity, but people use guns defensively (often without firing them) two and a half million times each year. As John Lott of the University of Chicago Law School points out, this number includes incidents in which mass shootings are prevented or curtailed and in which mothers thwart car-jackings when their children are in the cars.

Writes Lott in the July/August 1998 issue of *The American Enterprise*: "On the surface, [school shootings] seem to present a strong argument for restricting private gun ownership. But the truth is, guns wielded by private citizens have saved lives in such incidents, including some of the recent ones." He reminds us that the shooting spree at a Pearl, Mississippi, school earlier this year might have taken more victims had an assistant principal not retrieved a gun from his car and used it to hold the student assailant until the police appeared. A similar thing happened to end the student shooting incident at Edinboro, Pennsylvania.

The deaths that do not occur because lawful people have guns cannot be seen and therefore are not entered in the plus column of the ledger. If guns are banned, lawful people, not criminals, will be denied a key method of using force—in defense of self and others. Thus, more may die at the hands of criminals than do today.

We can demonstrate this negatively with a real incident. Some years ago, George Hennard, Jr., walked into Luby's Cafeteria in Killeen, Texas, and opened fire, killing 23 patrons and wounding 28 others. Suzanne Gratia Hupp was having lunch there with her parents and saw them murdered. It so happens that this woman usually carried a handgun in her purse (which at the time was illegal to do). But on this day, fearing revocation of a recently received occupational license, she left the gun in her car when she and her parents went into the cafeteria. She is convinced that if she had taken the gun with her, she would have stopped the shooter. Her parents, and others, might have been spared. They can be counted among the victims of gun control.

There is still another kind of "unseen" in the issue of gun control. A majority of states has now legalized the concealed carry of handguns for citizens who satisfy a few objective criteria. Formerly, local authorities had wide discretion in granting such permits. Where concealed carry is allowed, it is the criminals who are plagued by the unseen. They can't know who has a gun and who doesn't. This creates a free-rider problem—for the thugs. People who choose not to carry firearms nevertheless benefit from the fact that others may and do carry them. Criminals don't typically like to attack dangerous targets. Since criminals can't know in advance who's carrying and who isn't carrying a gun, they have to assume anyone might be—if not the potential victim, then someone nearby. That's how to create safety on the streets.

A world without any guns would not be safer than one in which lawful people were free to own them. Without guns, bigger, stronger thugs would have an advantage over smaller, weaker victims. Women, especially, would suffer. In that world, the unseen would be the victims of fatal beatings and stabbings who would have remained alive had they possessed firearms with which to defend themselves.

> *"LGBT clients of all ages are still likely to face coming-out issues, clinicians report. Young people, though, are more likely to face a host of post-coming-out problems, since many are likely to already have come out to their parents."*

Greater Acceptance Means the LGBTQ Community's Concerns Have Shifted Toward the Mainstream

Tori DeAngelis

In the following viewpoint Tori DeAngelis argues that psychological practitioners are seeing a new generation of concerns in their LGBTQ clients. The author penned this viewpoint in 2002. Readers should contemplate the relevance of her opinions and the issues she raises here under the backdrop of current events and views regarding the LGBTQ community. Have conditions improved to the point where coming out has become less of a problem or at least one that no longer requires psychological treatment? Has widespread acceptance of individual sexuality replaced skepticism and scorn? Or are the points raised here by the author still pertinent? Tori DeAngelis is a writer in Syracuse, New York.

"A New Generation of Issues for LGBT Clients," by Tori DeAngelis, American Psychological Association, February 2002. Reprinted by permission.

As you read, consider the following questions:

1. How have the issues regarding LGBTQ rights and their acceptance in the United States changed in the nearly two decades since the viewpoint was written?

2. Why is the author concerned about the relationships between kids and their LGBTQ parents?

3. Why does the author feel about the need for gay teenagers to reveal their sexual identities to their parents, according to the viewpoint?

In the 32 years since patrons of the Stonewall Inn challenged police who raided the now-famous gay nightclub, lesbians, gays and bisexuals have grown in personal and political power, creating their own communities and finding acceptance in traditional ones as well.

Conversations taking place in today's therapy offices reflect this change. Although many lesbian, gay, bisexual and transgendered (LGBT) people still bring issues of discrimination and fear of rejection to their psychologists' offices, they are just as likely to discuss such mainstream issues as parenting and fears about aging.

Meanwhile, new trends have emerged in therapy, too, as younger generations of LGBT people wrestle with problems such as a resurgence of HIV infection among gay male youth and changing identity issues. Likewise, groups that have been more closeted, including transsexuals and transgendered people, are finding their voice and appearing more often in treatment to work on identity and relationship concerns.

"Some issues haven't changed much at all since Stonewall, and others have changed dramatically," comments Doug Haldeman, PhD, a clinical faculty member at the University of Washington and an APA Council representative for Div. 44 (Society for the Psychological Study of Lesbian, Gay and Bisexual Issues). "People still need help with coming out—when, how and to whom. Some cultures within our culture are still very homophobic."

At the same time, Haldeman says, psychologists are seeing "a whole host of other issues related to the creation of LGBT families, LGBT people in the workplace, generational differences and the reality of multiple-minority identities—issues that demand our best research and clinical skills."

Generation Gaps

Psychologists working with LGBT clients are finding the need to tune in to generational differences, experts note—whether it's understanding young LGBT clients' new ways of thinking about their sexuality or assessing reasons for depression in older gay men.

Many LGBT youth, for instance, now call themselves "queer" as a blanket term for their community, and they're more likely to accept variations in their ranks than previous generations, says Beth Firestein, PhD, a private practitioner in Loveland, Colo., and editor of "Bisexuality: The Psychology and Politics of an Invisible Minority" (Sage, 1996), a compendium of research on bisexuality. In communities that include lesbians and bisexual women, for example, "there's more unity and community, cooperation and friendly relationships now than there was 10 or 15 years ago," she says.

Esther D. Rothblum, PhD, a professor of psychology at the University of Vermont, agrees it's more common for today's young LGBT people to express and accept fluid gender and sexual identities. "In the generation before mine, if you went to a lesbian bar and didn't identify as either butch or femme, they'd think you were an imposter," she says. "Now young lesbians are just as likely to say they feel butch one day and femme the next."

Another strong feature that distinguishes younger lesbians from their Baby Boomer counterparts is their lack of identification with the feminist movement, says sex therapist Suzanne Iasenza, PhD, a professor of counseling at the John Jay College of Criminal Justice in New York.

"Their attitude is, 'What does my sexuality have to do with politics?'" says Iasenza. "You're not likely to find them saying they're lesbian as a statement against patriarchy or because they don't like the way men take over their bodies or their lives."

Gay Men, Young and Aging

Some young gay men are presenting a serious challenge for practitioners. Since protease inhibitors were introduced in the mid-1990s, researchers have reported a surge in the number of young gay men who practice unsafe sex, known these days as "barebacking," in part because they thought the drugs would protect them from HIV's worst effects.

The events of Sept. 11 seem to have escalated this trend, with the crisis adding a dose of fatalism and nihilism to impulsiveness, according to Haldeman. As a consequence, Haldeman finds himself taking a hard line with these clients, despite his therapeutic training. He fears that if he doesn't push them to change, he'll see more young men with HIV who need help managing the disease.

Columbia University HIV-prevention researcher and clinician Alex Carballo-Dieguez, PhD, says that in addition to barebacking, he's spotting a body-image problem among his young gay clients. "Twenty years ago, your body image was about what you wore, how you wore your hair and so on," Carballo-Dieguez says. "Now, it's about the transformation of the body itself. These guys want to reshape their bodies to make them look a certain way"—muscled and perfectly toned. "A lot of times that's achieved with chemicals, hormones and even surgery," he says.

This obsession becomes especially problematic when it comes to partner-shopping, with clients looking for Mr. Right only if he's also Mr. Buff, Carballo-Dieguez says.

To combat this problem, he has clients walk through their own sexual and emotional histories and take a realistic look at themselves.

"They get to see that they've never been satisfied with the guys they score with," he says. "They're never certain that they're attractive enough or that the other person's attractive enough."

This insight can help them stop the appearance-obsessed merry-go-round, he says.

Gay men in their 40s and 50s also bring a "looks" challenge into therapy, says Haldeman.

"Middle-aged gay men face tremendous challenges because we grew up in such a youth-oriented gay culture," says Haldeman, who's 50. "Thirty-five is seen as old, and 50 is ancient! That's a blow to our narcissism. Not only are we not the pretty things when we walk into the bar, we're the age of the parents of the pretty things."

Haldeman urges such clients to take a life inventory, to look at the past and see what's valuable there. "They need to ask themselves, 'Am I on a path where, when I look back, I'll be satisfied with my life?'" he says.

The silver lining to their aging regrets: "Thank God we're aging," Haldeman adds. "We buried so many of our generation years ago. So we have a special joy and appreciation of life that we might not otherwise have had."

Coming Out, Parenting

LGBT clients of all ages are still likely to face coming-out issues, clinicians report. Young people, though, are more likely to face a host of post-coming-out problems, since many are likely to already have come out to their parents, says Marny Hall, PhD, a psychotherapist and researcher in the San Francisco Bay area. While that's often good news, she observes, often their parents' acceptance is conditional.

"Parents tend to display a sort of limited tolerance for their 'queer' kids—what I call tolerance without equality," Hall says. "The clients I see are constantly confronted with issues like this."

LGBT clients are also dealing with the flip side of that equation: being parents themselves. Many lesbians and gay men are the first generation of homosexuals to have children who are becoming teens. Some have found that while as younger children they had no problem accepting their gay parents, as they move into adolescence, some teens start to feel embarrassed by their parents' homosexuality, says Haldeman.

"Some young people are really conflicted and may try to hide the fact they have two same-sex parents by having the parents pick them up from school in some secret location," he says—dynamics that affect the child's relationship with parents and peers and the parents' relationship.

Another spin on the parenting issue is that today, gays and lesbians have children not only from dissolved heterosexual marriages, but from broken-up gay relationships as well, Hall adds. Conflicts involving children of same-sex unions present particular difficulties because the legal ground for same-sex couples and their child-custody rights "is shifting all the time," she says.

"When there are no clear guidelines, what often substitutes are conflicts within the couple," Hall says. "Relationship problems can really get played out in this arena."

Psychologists are helping these clients separate parenting problems from relationship problems and devising solutions that don't require legal structures to implement, she says.

Gender-Blending and Fluid Identities

A final theme clinicians report in their practices is more questioning and fluidity around gender identity and sexual attraction. While these issues are central in the lives of transsexuals or transgendered people, others are questioning these elements of identity and expression too, therapists report.

"I'd put a fifth category on the end of 'LGBT'—a 'Q' for 'questioning,'" says Hall. "Gender identity and sexual identity issues have frayed more and more around the edges."

On one hand, there's a push for LGBT young people to come out at earlier ages, she notes; on the other, more young people are pausing indefinitely in what she calls the "lingering" category. "There are no more givens about gender identity," she says. "Young people don't take sexual identity for granted."

Bisexuals represent another group that turns conventional thinking on its head, says Firestein.

"Often bisexuals want to label themselves as lesbian or gay because occupying a middle ground is so difficult in a culture that dichotomizes sexual orientation and gender identity," she says. Conventional thinking has it that if bisexuals are attracted to people of both sexes, they must have more than one partner, and that defies society's value on monogamy. Bisexuals tend to internalize this social tension, Firestein says, so a common therapeutic question is, "If I identify as bisexual, what does that mean about my choice of partners?"

To help bisexual clients face this concern, Firestein conducts an exercise demonstrating that the number of partners you have and your sexual orientation exist on different dimensions. As two examples, you can be monogamous and bisexual, and you can be heterosexual and have more than one sexual partner.

For transsexuals—people who have nontraditional gender identity or expression—issues include coming to terms with their feelings about their true gender and then deciding whether and how to act on those feelings. In her work with transgendered people, New York City private practitioner and gender expert Katherine Rachlin, PhD, notes that transgendered people struggle not so much with who they are as with finding ways to fit into a society that doesn't understand them. She says that transgendered people, who do not identify as either male or female, sometimes work on accepting a fluid gender identity. More often, Rachlin says, they choose to identify as one gender or the other because it's too challenging to live in a gender-dichotomous society otherwise.

Therapy with transgendered people requires extra education and perception, Rachlin believes. She spent hundreds of hours with this community before she had a good understanding of how to work with "trans" clients, she says. For clinicians who want to work with trans people, she recommends reading the Harry Benjamin Foundation's "Standards of care for the treatment of gender identity disorders," available on the Web at www.HBIGDA.org.

The document outlines the role of the therapist and describes the qualifications needed to be a gender specialist.

In her 15 years of being involved with the trans community, Rachlin has appreciated learning a new and different way of looking at gender.

"There's a great mystery that underlies transgenderism, and it does change the way you see the world," she says. "I had to redefine male and female, man and woman, for myself. These concepts are now disproven to me."

"Corporate America has stepped into the vacuum of state protection. Some 91 per cent of Fortune 500 companies mention sexual orientation in their non-discrimination policies."

There Is a Generation Gap in the Fight for LGBTQ Rights

Josh Spero

In the following viewpoint Josh Spero argues that the LGBTQ community is experiencing growing pains in the fight for civil rights. The author notes the economics of acceptance and how the hiring of those with nontraditional sexual identities can have a positive impact on the financial health of a society. He also expresses a view that a strong workplace environment can provide a sanctuary for those who face negativity for their sexual identities in their personal lives. Josh Spero is deputy editor of the special reports section of the Financial Times.

As you read, consider the following questions:

1. How do different generations of LGBTQ people vary in their outlooks and identification, according to the author?
2. How have American companies created a more inviting environment for potential LGBTQ employees?
3. Why does the author compare the professional expectations of straight Americans to those of LGBTQ workers?

The fight for LGBT rights has taken different forms across generations. In 1969, it was truly a fight—a series of riots outside the Stonewall Inn, a New York gay bar. In 2003, campaigners won a political battle when the UK government established the Employment Equality regulations, banning discrimination against workers on the grounds of sexual orientation. In 2015, judicial confrontation culminated in the US Supreme Court legalising gay marriage.

This patchwork accretion of rights and protections gained over the past 50 years means there are LGBT people working today who remember a time when homosexuality was illegal and being able to marry their partner a distant fantasy. Job security for LGBT people who began their careers in the 1960s and 1970s was far from assured and coming out as trans was downright dangerous. Contrarily, there are people starting work today who have come of age as lesbian, gay, bisexual and trans acceptance has soared in society.

Richard Easton, 55, a shop manager at J Sainsbury who has worked for the UK supermarket chain for 36 years, remembers when being out at work was unthinkable. "It was something most people didn't talk about in those days," he says. "If you were gay, you were pigeonholed [as camp]." There was a "very, very small" gay community at the company, he adds, and that was not vocal.

Antony Smith, equalities officer at charity Age UK, says for the older people he talks to advancements won in recent decades

MILLENNIALS ARE ABANDONING RELIGION

A couple of decades ago, when young adults began showing their dissatisfaction with organized religion by voting with their feet, it was fashionable for pundits to say this was happening because those religions weren't conservative or demanding enough.

Because the exodus was initially most pronounced among liberal, "mainline" Protestants like Episcopalians and Presbyterians, it was easy to point at liberalism as the root of the problem.

If churches just held fast to their standards, the thinking went, they would be fine, because strictness was what the masses secretly wanted. People craved firm boundaries. Conservatives, you will not be surprised to hear, were the most ardent supporters of this "strict churches" theory, which assured them they were already doing the most important things right.

But now the "strict churches" theory is crumbling because some strict denominations are themselves charting losses, or at least slower growth. The Southern Baptists have lost more than a million members over the last decade, according to LifeWay. Giving and attendance are down, and Southern Baptists are seeing more gray and silver heads in the pews.

were once "unimaginable". Those who came of age in the 1950s and 1960s "have lived through enormous change—and change that was probably unexpected." This means they are less likely to take the progress in LGBT inclusion for granted and more likely to worry about the possibility that it could be reversed.

Mr. Easton's story bears this out. In 2011, aged 50, he came out, with "no negative feedback at all" and five years later he recorded a clip for a corporate film about diversity. Despite the company's embrace, he is unsure the acceptance will last. He is an advocate for policies and networks that support LGBT people, not least in terms of visibility. He says only "constant vigilance" can stop a slide back into ignorance.

Meanwhile, the Church of Jesus Christ of Latter-day Saints has seen its once-enviable U.S. growth rate slow to under 1 percent in each of the last two years. Mormonism, which grew by just .75 percent in this country in 2017, is barely keeping pace with the growth of the U.S. population (+.71 percent). That's down from a 2 percent Mormon growth rate in 2001, 3.1 percent in 1987 and 5.4 percent in 1960.

Now it's liberal pundits who are quick to point the finger. A *HuffPost* headline last year screeched that "Evangelical Christianity's Big Turn-Off" was its relentless pursuit of a conservative political agenda. Let's call this the "alienation" theory, which says that churches that have waged war against LGBT rights or supported Donald Trump are reaping the fallout: Millennials want nothing to do with them.

There's evidence to support the alienation theory, to a point. Young adults are leaving religion in droves, and some of it is related to politics. People who vote or lean Democratic are more likely to be "nones," defined as people who have no religious affiliation. They're not all atheists. About one-third of U.S. nones say religion is somewhat or very important in their lives and most say they believe in God, though the percentage holding theistic beliefs is falling.

"Why Millennials Are Really Leaving Religion (It's Not Just Politics, Folks)," by Jana Riess, Religion & Ethics NewsWeekly, July 16, 2018.

His worries about the fragility of LGBT rights appear well founded. In the US, a majority of states do not have workplace protection for LGBT people. This year North Carolina and Georgia passed bills that effectively banned or invalidated such protections. The Georgia bill, which was ultimately vetoed by the state's governor, "would have ended our protections before we even had them", says Jeff Graham, executive director of advocacy group Georgia Equality.

Corporate America has stepped into the vacuum of state protection. Some 91 per cent of Fortune 500 companies mention sexual orientation in their non-discrimination policies, according to the Human Rights Campaign, an LGBT advocacy group.

UK companies are following suit. In the 13 years that the British campaign group Stonewall has run its programme to teach corporate best practice, membership has grown from fewer than 50 businesses to more than 700. Unlike Stonewall's more secretive initial members, its cohort of companies today see significant benefit in being "out and proud."

Not all generations feel the same way. For older workers, coming out after decades of hiding their true selves can feel awkward and frightening, especially if they were part of the workforce before 2003, when employers could fire openly gay staff.

For Generation X and millennials—born between the mid-1960s and the mid-1990s—coming out can be uncomfortable for a different reason. Ruth Hunter, 39, a director at consultancy PwC, plays down being gay. "It's not the only thing or the main thing about me," she says.

Many millennials intensely dislike being labelled. Kate Clark, 25, a technology project manager at Sainsbury's, says she has a girlfriend at the moment but "I don't put myself in any of the boxes." Similarly, Nick Pringle, 24, a senior associate at PwC, says, "I don't want to be known as 'the gay one.'" However, as his work is project-based, he ends up "coming out again and again and again" to new teams, which can be "frustrating" if innocuous.

While Mr. Easton, part of the baby-boomer generation, is more worried about rights being rolled back, Mr. Pringle focuses on their expansion through the company and beyond. He sees the usefulness of a corporate LGBT policy as a safety net and because it "sets the tone in the culture." Such responses follow quite naturally, it might be argued, from the different climates of LGBT acceptance within which Mr. Easton and Mr. Pringle came of age.

What is perhaps surprising, given today's corporate culture of tolerance, at least in the west, is that millennials often go back into the closet when they start their first job, says Deena Fidas of the HRC. She believes this happens because companies do not give out "the clear message" that recruits should "bring their full self to work." Despite this, LGBT youths in the US have almost equally high expectations for their careers as their straight counterparts. An HRC survey found 92 per cent of young members of the LGBT community believe they can have a good job compared with 95 per cent of straight youths.

Outside the corporate sector, some workplaces put less focus on sexual orientation. Syma Khalid, professor of computational biophysics at Southampton university, has discussed LGBT rights with colleagues old and young. The prevailing view has been that in academia, sexual identity is unimportant. Academics are "an odd bunch," she says, more concerned with papers published or grants won than personal lives. "There is a collegiate atmosphere in general and a cerebral element to it."

In academia or beyond, work can provide a refuge, especially in countries hostile to the LGBT community and for trans individuals who find it difficult to be accepted at home.

Prof Khalid says work can offer a "second family," a more accepting one, and if work is the only place you are out, then companies ought to ensure they offer the best atmosphere possible.

> *"Respect for nature is fundamental. Governments must protect ecosystems key to the fight against climate change: rivers, wetlands, oceans, forests and mangroves absorb large quantities of carbon, slowing warming."*

The Planet Is Worth Fighting For

Laura Yaniz

In the following viewpoint Laura Yaniz offers straightforward ideas that governments can utilize to combat climate change that extend beyond what individuals can do on a daily basis. Included among her suggestions are protecting and restoring key ecosystems, promoting green energy, and combating climate pollutants. Those ideas have been bandied about for years. Yaniz stresses their importance here and provides some concrete tactics that would allow governments to carry out the objectives. Laura Yaniz is a freelance writer and social media content editor.

"5 Ways Our Governments Can Confront Climate Change," by Laura Yaniz, AIDA, November 17, 2017. Reprinted by permission.

As you read, consider the following questions:

1. Which tactic to combat climate change do you consider most effective?
2. Do you feel all five of these ideas cited in the viewpoint will be embraced by a US government controlled by either Democrats or Republicans?
3. Does the author provide compelling arguments for the need to take action on climate change?

As individuals, we know about the small actions we can take to help reduce the emissions that cause climate change. But what can and should our governments do, seeing as their large-scale actions are fundamental to the welfare of their people?

Earth, we have a problem: we're essentially melting.

High rates of greenhouse gas emissions, paired with environmental degradation and the overexploitation of natural resources, have us in a race against time. Ninety-seven percent of scientists agree that climate change is a result of human activities. And if we fail to stop global warming soon, the changes will be catastrophic.

Each year, at the United Nations climate conference, global leaders meet to discuss actions we can take to help prevent, and be better prepared for, climate change. At COP21 the first binding global climate accord, the Paris Agreement, was born. This year, during COP23, delegates seek to establish rules to allow for its proper implementation.

As individuals, most of us understand what we can do to reduce emissions: save energy, use the car less, recycle more, make better consumption choices, and engage in family planning.

But what can our governments do? To discuss their contribution is to talk about large-scale measures that are vital to ensuring a better future for all.

1. Protect and Restore Key Ecosystems

Respect for nature is fundamental. Governments must protect ecosystems key to the fight against climate change: rivers, wetlands, oceans, forests and mangroves absorb large quantities of carbon, slowing warming. Mangroves also serve as a barrier against tropical storms, and wetlands absorb excess water from floods, both extreme weather events exacerbated by climate change.

"Healing the natural system is the most feasible, realistic and fair option, since it would benefit humanity and all species," said Florencia Ortúzar, an attorney with AIDA's Climate Change Program. "In terms of conservation and restoration, we're in a race against time, and we're already beginning to witness alarming natural phenomena, like forests so degraded they're losing their ability to absorb carbon."

2. Support Small Agricultural Producers

According to the FAO, the meat industry is responsible for 15 to 18 percent of all greenhouse gas emissions, exceeding even those of the transportation sector. In addition, it is the most significant source of water use and contamination in the world. Today, 80 percent of all agricultural production goes toward feeding animals not people. The expansion of land for livestock, and the crops to feed them, is the most significant cause of deforestation in the Amazon.

Governments can make a difference by supporting small local producers who, unlike large factory farms, employ sustainable practices, care about land restoration, benefit nearby communities, and make animals and crops more resilient to climate change. It's less about everybody becoming vegetarians, but more about supporting those who produce our food with a respect for nature.

3. Promote Green Energy

Thirty-five percent of all global emissions come from energy production. But as countries bet on more development, they're also betting on more energy production. But as countries bet on more development, they're also betting on more energy.

While thermoelectric and hydroelectric energies were long considered the cheapest options, technological developments have allowed us to find better, cheaper, more efficient alternatives. With proper long-term planning, nations can avoid old climate-aggravating energy sources (hydropower is not green) and opt for small wind, solar, geothermal, oceanic and other projects that adapt to a place's unique characteristics.

"When thinking about energy, it's best to bet on a diversified matrix, prioritizing projects that are close to places where people need energy, saving on losses and infrastructure," Ortúzar explained. "We must give absolute priority to the protection of nature. Every action, public policy, or strategy should be analyzed with nature in mind, and the production of energy is a good starting point."

4. Combat Short-Lived Climate Pollutants

Carbon dioxide (CO_2) is the most infamous greenhouse gas. Since it remains in the atmosphere for centuries (even millennia), even if we stopped all its emissions sources today, the effects of climate change would continue. The good news is that other contaminants exist that contribute to climate change and only last a few days or years in the atmosphere. They're known as short-lived climate pollutants, and they're responsible for 30 to 45 percent of the emissions that cause global warming.

These pollutants include black carbon (soot), methane, ozone, and the hydro fluorocarbons found in refrigerants. Their effective control, through national policies and regulations, could accelerate the fight against climate change in the short term. In addition, because they cause serious air pollution, measures to mitigate them would directly benefit human health.

5. Bet on Adaptation, Not Just Mitigation

In the fight against climate change, work aimed at reducing emissions, stopping their effects and diminishing future consequences is known as mitigation. It is important. However, some communities are already experiencing tragic consequences due to changes in climate over a short period of time. So we also must act to prevent catastrophes, increase resilience, and reduce vulnerability, which is known as adaptation.

Projects to mitigate emissions are more attractive financially than those designed for adaptation, which are generally focused on the most vulnerable communities. But it is important to give adaptation the significance it deserves in recognition of the fact that the impacts of climate change are already a grave reality for many.

At this year's COP, representatives are discussing a "loss and damage" mechanism, referring to the compensation that developed countries—the main causes of climate change—must make to developing countries, which suffer significant losses due to adverse climate effects, Ortúzar explained. Our governments must support these discussions and commit to the effective use of resources, so all the world's people can be better prepared for, and help to prevent, greater changes to our climate.

> *"Now seven months into his presidency, Trump has pushed for dramatic changes to the nation's immigration system. But he's also been stymied by Congress and by the courts."*

The Country Is Divided on Immigration

Scott Horsley, Joel Rose, and Jim Zarroli

In the following viewpoint Scott Horsley, Joel Rose, and Jim Zarroli examine a series of misleading statements or blatant lies uttered by Donald Trump during his presidential campaign and his time in the White House, on his plans to combat illegal immigration. The authors cite a number of threats made by Trump to satisfy his base that he either had no intention of carrying out or were simply unrealistic, including the infamous promise to build a great wall on the border and force Mexico to pay for it. Scott Horsley is NPR's chief economics correspondent. Joel Rose covers immigration and breaking news for NPR's national desk. Jim Zarroli covers economics and business news for NPR.

As you read, consider the following questions:

1. Do the authors believe Donald Trump has taken an effective approach to combat illegal immigration?
2. What are the authors trying to say about the president's honesty?
3. Do the viewpoint authors provide strong evidence to make their points?

President Trump returns Tuesday night to the same Phoenix convention center where he spoke during the campaign last year, laying out a 10-point plan to fight illegal immigration.

He's also visiting a US Customs and Border Protection facility in Yuma, Ariz., a few miles from the Southwest border.

Now seven months into his presidency, Trump has pushed for dramatic changes to the nation's immigration system. But he's also been stymied by Congress and by the courts.

Here's a look at what the Trump White House has accomplished on each of those 10 promises—and what it hasn't.

1. "We will build a great wall along the southern border. And Mexico will pay for the wall."

The border wall remains more aspiration than reality. The Department of Homeland Security is waiving environmental rules to speed up construction of prototypes near San Diego.

But so far, Mexico has balked at paying for the wall. And so has Congress. The House has appropriated nearly $1.6 billion for the first phase of construction, but the Senate hasn't.

2. "We are going to end catch and release."

Administration officials say they're following through on Trump's promise to end so-called catch and release. That's how many critics describe the policy that allowed many immigrants to go free until their court dates, which can often be years away because of court backlogs.

In practice, it's not clear that the Trump administration is handling these cases much differently than previous administrations did.

But there has been a dramatic drop in the number of people apprehended at the Southwest border since Trump took office—a 46 percent drop during the first seven months of the year compared to 2016, according to a DHS official. The total for March was the lowest in at least 17 years, although the numbers have started to creep back up since then.

3. "Zero tolerance for criminal aliens."

Immigration and Customs Enforcement (ICE) arrests are up more than 43 percent since late January compared to the same period in 2016, according to a DHS official. "We are still continuing to prioritize our resources on those individuals that create and pose the greatest public safety and national security threat," the official said. Seventy-two percent of those arrested had criminal convictions, a much lower percentage than the final years of the Obama administration.

Trump has pushed Congress for funding to hire more agents for ICE and US Customs and Border Protection. But like funding for the border wall, Congress has yet to sign off.

4. "Block funding for sanctuary cities."

The Justice Department is trying to follow through on that promise to punish so-called sanctuary cities, which limit cooperation with federal immigration authorities. DOJ made some law enforcement grants contingent on whether those cities do more to help ICE.

But Chicago and California quickly took the administration to court. That's in addition to lawsuits filed earlier this year by San Francisco, Seattle and other self-described sanctuary cities.

5. "Cancel unconstitutional executive orders and enforce all immigration laws."

This probably refers to two Obama-era executive actions including DACA, which protects undocumented immigrants who were brought to the country as children from deportation.

The Trump White House dropped its support for a related program called DAPA, which was supposed to help the parents of those children.

But so far, the White House has allowed DACA to continue, much to the dismay of immigration hard-liners. Texas and other states are threatening to sue if the administration doesn't pull its support for DACA by Sept. 5.

6. "We are going to suspend the issuance of visas to any place where adequate screening cannot occur."

This is part of what Trump's travel ban executive order was supposed to do.

The order Trump signed just a week after taking office would have blocked travelers from seven mostly Muslim countries that the administration says are known havens for terrorists.

Federal courts put the original order on hold. But the Supreme Court allowed a limited version of the travel ban to take effect until it can hear legal challenges to the ban in the fall.

7. "We will ensure that other countries take their people back when we order them deported."

Trump pointed out in Phoenix last year that immigrants with criminal records can wind up staying in the US because their home country won't take them back. The White House has reportedly cut the number of non-cooperative countries from 23 to 12. Immigration hawks say that's a big win, and that the administration deserves more credit for it.

8. "We will finally complete the biometric entry-exit visa tracking system which we need desperately."

For years, Congress has required the Department of Homeland Security to create a system to track everyone who comes in and out of the country using biometric technologies like facial recognition or fingerprint scanners.

In recent years, a majority of new undocumented immigrants have overstayed temporary visas, while the number crossing the border illegally has fallen.

Customs and Border Protection is testing a few prototype systems at US airports this summer. But experts say a comprehensive solution that will work at more than 300 land, sea and air ports of entry remains a long way off.

9. "We will turn off the jobs and benefits magnet."

In the spring, Trump signed an executive order directing federal agencies to "Buy American" and "Hire American," and urging others to do the same.

But critics point out that Trump's own companies continue to hire foreign guest workers and manufacture overseas. And just as the White House's "Made in America" week was underway in July, the administration announced it would allow an additional 15,000 temporary foreign workers.

10. "We will reform legal immigration to serve the best interests of America and its workers, the forgotten people."

Earlier this month, the White House threw its support behind the RAISE Act, which would prioritize immigrants with valuable skills and high-paying US job offers, and gradually reduce the number of other foreign nationals who can reunite with their families already living in the US. But there seems to be little enthusiasm for the bill in the Senate.

Periodical and Internet Sources Bibliography

The following articles have been selected to supplement the diverse views presented in this chapter.

Anthony Cilluffo and D'Vera Cohn, "7 Demographic Trends Shaping the US and the World in 2018," Pew Research Center, April 24, 2018. https://www.pewresearch.org/fact-tank/2018/04/25/7-demographic-trends-shaping-the-u-s-and-the-world-in-2018/.

Ryan D. Enos, "How Segregation Leads to Racist Voting by Whites," Vox, November 28, 2017. https://www.vox.com/the-big-idea/2017/11/28/16707438/social-geography-trump-rise-segregation-psychology-racism.

Umair Irfan, "Americans Are Worried about Climate Change—but Don't Want to Pay Much to Fix It," Vox, January 28, 2019. https://www.vox.com/2019/1/28/18197262/climate-change-poll-public-opinion-carbon-tax.

Ayana Elizabeth Johnson, "Young Voters and Voters of Color Are Key to Climate Policy," The Hill, September 8, 2018. https://thehill.com/opinion/energy-environment/405753-young-voters-and-voters-of-color-are-key-to-halting-climate-change.

Ezra Klein, "White Threat in a Browning America," Vox, July 30, 2018. https://www.vox.com/policy-and-politics/2018/7/30/17505406/trump-obama-race-politics-immigration.

Kari Paul, "The Vast Majority of Young Americans Favor Stricter Gun Control," Market Watch, October 28, 2018. https://www.marketwatch.com/story/the-vast-majority-of-millennials-favor-gun-control-2017-10-27.

Monica Duffy Toft, "White Right? How Demographics Is Changing US Politics," The Conversation, January 7, 2019. https://theconversation.com/white-right-how-demographics-is-changing-us-politics-107872.

Jonathan Vespa, David M. Armstrong, and Lauren Medina, "Demographic Turning Points for the United States: Population Projections for 2020 to 2060," Current Population Reports, P25-1144, US Census Bureau. https://www.census.gov/content/dam/Census/library/publications/2018/demo/P25_1144.pdf.

OPPOSING
VIEWPOINTS®
SERIES

CHAPTER 2

How Will Its Aging Population Impact the United States?

Chapter Preface

A mong the most challenging tasks placed upon any society at any time is caring for the elderly. But currently, in the early decades of the twenty-first century, the United States is faced with a monumental responsibility, as the huge number of baby boomers place a strain on its health care system. Will the aged be able to afford the enormous cost of health care through government programs such as Medicare and Social Security? Will there be enough health care professionals to staff hospitals, assisted living facilities, and nursing homes that will house the elderly and sick?

The workforce, too, has been impacted by shifting demographics. The baby boomer generation has stayed in the workplace far longer than their predecessors, causing a lack of opportunities for the generations behind it. What will happen as that generation retires and jobs need to be filled?

Another impact of an aging population will fall into the political realm. Despite the noted liberalism of many baby boomers in the 1960s and 1970s, those from that generation—especially among the white population—are considered far more conservative than young Americans in general. One wonders if conservative baby boomers will remain politically active in seeking a counterbalance against the emerging liberalism or at least will continue to vote conservatively in future elections. The baby boomer generation born after World War II was among the largest in US history and will continue to make a major impact on the United States politically for two or more decades.

The following chapter addresses issues facing and regarding an aging population with a focus on health care and the workforce. Can baby boomers who remain actively working adapt to new technology and an uncertain labor market? And can younger generations fill their very large shoes as more boomers retire? The viewpoints that follow explore those issues.

> *"We need care delivery and payment models that provide safe and cost efficient health care and that will address access for the staggering numbers of aging boomers who have or will develop very complex care needs."*

Baby Boomers Are Disrupting US Health Care

Willis Towers Watson

In the following viewpoint staff writers from Willis Towers Watson argue that health care professionals and decision makers will face enormous challenges in the future, particularly regarding health issues facing an aging baby boomer population. The authors give advice as to how best to ensure available and effective treatment. They caution that medical advances have allowed Americans to live longer on average than ever before and that the health care industry must keep up. Willis Towers Watson is a global multinational risk management, insurance brokerage, and advisory company.

As you read, consider the following questions:

1. How can the economic health of the United States be negatively affected by a strain on the health care system, according to the viewpoint?

2. What is different about the baby boomer generation from previous generations as they head into retirement and old age?

3. Do you believe the viewpoint provides an optimistic or pessimistic view of the nation's capability to provide for the increasing number of elderly patients?

The approximately 78 million American baby boomers are causing disruption in health care. As three million of them hit retirement age every year, they will continue to require health care services for decades to come. Not all baby boomers are old enough for Medicare benefits. Providers and payors must effectively manage the health of this population that uses more resources per person than past generations. They will have to address care across all settings, including hospitals, ambulatory care, aging services, home health and telehealth.

Keep in mind "members" of any generation are all different, and not all persons in a "population" are motivated by the same events and subjectivities the public may use when referring to boomers, Generation X, Generation Y, etc.

The Centers for Disease Control and Prevention (CDC) shared that Americans are living longer than at any other time. A recent study (October 2016) by the Society of Actuaries provided a "best guess" that the average 65-year-old man should die a few months short of his 86th birthday and a woman at 88. But researchers have also found that despite this improvement in life expectancy the boomers are less healthy than previous generations. CDC data has seen a continuous increase in chronic health conditions since 2012 in this age group. These conditions include cancer, heart disease, hypertension, dementia, arthritis, depression, obesity and diabetes. This all combines to place further pressures on our fragile health systems.

Many feel that, just like children have specialists (pediatricians), older people should have access to professionals trained in caring for them for the same reasons. This does not mean that every practitioner must be a gerontologist but at a minimum should have the competencies to address the unique health care needs of an aging, older population. At the same time boomers are transitioning in their lives, so are a significant number of health care providers, including physicians and nurses. Demand exceeds supply in an already stressed care continuum. Baby boomers will lead the advancement of alternative methods for monitoring health and providing care that will allow improvement in health management of generations to follow.

What Other Factors Are Impacting Baby Boomers?

Studies continue to show that this generation is less well-off financially. This includes preparedness for retirement and how they will access and pay for health care during this transition. What are some of the contributing factors?

- The 2008 recession negatively impacted boomers
- Many lost money or could not relocate because of changes in real estate values
  - Upside down on mortgages
  - Lost equity and foreclosures
  - Parents of boomers with real estate also affected
- As companies "right sized," many boomers found themselves un- or under-employed
  - This impacted saving and retirement portfolios
- Many boomers are supporting others
  - Their own children (non-adult, adults living away and adults living with them)

- Grandchildren support or raising them
- Aged parents support or living with them

What Can Be Done?

Health care is often costly, fraught with quality issues and does not always meet the expectations of payors and users. Innovative care delivery models that engage the patient, caregivers, clinicians and care coordinators in a collaborative structure using assessment, option discussions, an understanding of costs and benefits and goal achievement support must be in place to successfully manage the baby boomer population. What should be considered?

- Improving engagement in wellness and prevention efforts
- Reconfirming adherence to medications and medical advice
- Patient and/or care provider assessment for communication and comprehension barriers
- Managing chronic conditions and disabilities
- Reducing unnecessary test and procedures—while differentiating the message from denial of care
- Evaluate the benefits of offering a geriatric emergency department
- Many boomers are supporting others
- Better managing advanced or terminal illness and improving aging in place and end of life decision making
- Health care providers should be augmenting their elder care medical knowledge and skill sets
- Providers need to evaluate their own workforce staffing to meet demand and achieve access

  - Health care providers are experiencing their own crisis with an extremely large number of nurses, physicians and other clinicians exiting the workforce at the same time baby boomers are placing a substantial demand for access (remember not all baby boomers are old enough for Medicare)

Aging Population and Professional Liability Claims

In their 2016 "Healthcare Malpractice Claims" update, AIG devoted a section to "The Graying of America and the Impact of Elder Care." Also included were findings from elder care claims resolved by AIG between January 2012 and June of 2016.

The United States cannot afford to ignore how baby boomers are impacting health care. We need care delivery and payment models that provide safe and cost efficient health care and that will address access for the staggering numbers of aging boomers who have or will develop very complex care needs. Providers and payors also must realize that with this demand from a specific "at-risk" population, they also must assess their increased financial and liability exposures and impacts to their strategic plan.

"Because the vast majority of the new enrollees would be younger and healthier than current Medicare participants, the cost per person would be much less."

Medicare for All Could Be Cheaper Than We Think

Gerald Friedman

In the following viewpoint Gerald Friedman argues that "Medicare for All," a plan espoused by presidential candidate Bernie Sanders and other liberal politicians and embraced by many Americans but considered far too expensive and socialistic by others, should be considered seriously. Friedman contends that Medicare for All and a single-payer system would not only provide health care to every American but would do so affordably. The author explains how such savings can be achieved. Gerald Friedman is professor of economics at the University of Massachusetts, Amherst.

As you read, consider the following questions:

1. Does the author make a strong argument that Medicare for All would be affordable?
2. How does the author use the health care systems of other countries to make his case?
3. Why do you believe Medicare for All is such a critical topic in American political debate?

Public support for single-payer health care has been rising in recent months amid failed Republican efforts to repeal and replace the Affordable Care Act.

That's perhaps why Sen. Bernie Sanders on September 13 introduced a new version of his single-payer plan with the support of 16 Democratic colleagues, a sharp rise from 2013 when none signed on to a similar proposal. It would not only expand Medicare to all Americans but make it more comprehensive by covering more services like mental health, dental care and vision, all without copayments or deductibles.

But Sanders's plan would come at a steep price: likely more than US$14 trillion over the first decade, based on an estimate I did of a previous version.

There is, however, a simpler and less costly path toward single-payer, and it may have a better chance of success: Simply strike the words "who are age 65 or over" from the 1965 amendments to the Social Security Act that created Medicare and, voila, everyone (who wants) would be covered by the existing Medicare program.

While this wouldn't be single-payer—in which the government covers all health care costs—and private insurers would continue to operate alongside Medicare, it would be a substantial improvement over the current system.

I have been researching the economics of health care for four decades. While I prefer a more comprehensive universal health care plan that covers all Americans, a simpler version would be much more affordable—and maybe even politically possible.

What Medicare Was and What It Was Meant to Be

Striking the words "over 65" from the Medicare statutes was an idea championed by the late Senator Daniel Moynihan. Moynihan, who held several roles in the Kennedy and Johnson administrations, was an original architect of the War on Poverty and a central figure in the evolution of health care policy in the latter 20th century.

In fact, many advocates originally intended that Medicare be the basis for universal health insurance. A key reason it serves so well as the foundation is that it includes a funding mechanism—the 2.9 percent Medicare payroll tax paid by you and your employer, alongside modest monthly premiums.

In addition, its limited scope, skimpy benefits and cost-sharing keep costs low. Medicare covers only a little more than half of participants' health care spending, forcing many elderly Americans to buy private insurance and pay significant out-of-pocket expenses. A little over 11 million poorer participants also rely on Medicaid, especially for long-term care.

For example, Medicare covers hospitalization only after a person has paid the $1,316 deductible, and there's a copay of $329 per day after 60 days and double that beyond 90. It also covers only 80 percent of the cost of doctor visits and the use of medical equipment—though only after a $183 deductible and the monthly $134 premium.

Still, it provides meaningful protection against the potentially crippling cost of accident or illness.

Giving Medicare to Everyone

Single-payer, in its purest form, means the government becomes everyone's insurer, and private insurance is largely dropped as redundant. This is the way health insurance is provided in the United Kingdom and Canada, as well as other countries like Taiwan. Sanders's plan would follow this framework.

A simple expansion of Medicare would be more like a hybrid system in which the government program exists alongside private insurers, with residents free to use any combination of the two.

One of the reasons single-payer health care has failed in the United States is that even though it might eventually lower costs, it would require substantial new taxes up front. Sanders's plan, as I noted earlier, would cost around $1.4 trillion a year. But because of its lower benefit levels and built-in revenue stream, a simple Medicare expansion would cost substantially less, maybe only half that.

In 2015, the last year with complete data, over 55 million Americans received Medicare benefits (including nine million who were disabled). Total spending was $646 billion that year, or an average of $11,000 per recipient.

A simple expansion would add the nondisabled population under age 65 to Medicare: 28 million without insurance, 61 million covered by Medicaid or the Children's Health Insurance Plan and 181 million with private insurance. For the purposes of my calculations, I assume everyone eligible for Medicare would take advantage of the program.

Because the vast majority of the new enrollees would be younger and healthier than current Medicare participants, the cost per person would be much less, or about $5,527 for the once uninsured and $3,593 for everyone else. With a few other calculations, the total price tag of an expansion would tally around $836 billion—almost $600 billion less than Sanders's single-payer.

Substantial Savings

Something that often gets lost in the debate over the cost of single-payer is that its implementation would lead to a host of savings that make the bill to taxpayers a lot less than the sticker price.

I estimate that a full single-payer system would likely save almost 19 percent of current spending, or about $665 billion for 2017. A simple Medicare expansion wouldn't save quite as much but it'd still be significant.

So where would the savings come from?

To begin with, studies show that medical billing is more expensive in the US than in many countries.

THE EMERGING FIELD OF GERIATRICS

Medical students in the US today are the future face of the American health care system. As they study to become doctors, nurses and medical assistants, those interested in a career in health care should be aware of how the aging population in the US will change the medical industry, and how to provide the best care for their elderly patients. The medical practice of caring for seniors is known as geriatrics, and while there are tenets of this practice that are unique to the field, the basic elements can be used by any practitioner to ensure they are giving their patient the best care possible.

Medical assistants and doctors caring for elderly patients often work on interdisciplinary teams of other providers. Physicians, nurses, social workers, occupational therapists and family members all collaborate to provide comprehensive care for these patients with multiple needs.

Medical students today are being prepared to treat a wide variety of illnesses amongst a more diverse population than ever before. Older patients are a major portion of those who will be seeking medical care in the future. According to the American Medical Student Association, the population of individuals over the age of 65 will increase by 73 percent between 2010 and 2030, meaning one in five Americans will be a senior citizen. Medical students in all fields should be well-versed in the various chronic conditions that can befall seniors today. However, the need for medical assistants and doctors to focus their care solely on seniors is growing. According to a study conducted by the Alliance for Aging Research, 33,000 geriatricians will be needed by 2030, and currently there are only 8,800 practitioners that are certified.

Individuals born between the years 1946 and 1964 are categorized as baby boomers, according to the US Census Bureau. Approximately 75 million Americans make up the baby boom generation, and every year for the next 20 years roughly 3 million baby boomers will reach retirement age. These facts will drastically change society, public policy and health care as Americans' needs evolve and boomers leave the workforce in growing numbers. The boomer generation's sheer size is likely to capture the attention of providers and hospitals. Hospitals have to focus on both how to care for the aging population and how an aging health care workforce will affect services rendered.

"How Baby Boomers Will Affect the Health Care Industry in the U.S.," Carrington College, February 1, 2014.

The US health care system spends twice as much as Canada, for example, because more "payers" means more complexity. Savings from a simple Medicare expansion could reduce this waste by about $89 billion a year.

Another source of savings is on insurance administration. Private insurers spend more than 12 percent of total expenditures on overhead, compared with around 2 percent for Medicare. Savings from moving everyone to Medicare would approach around $75 billion because of economies of scale, lower managerial salaries and more meager marketing expense.

A third way a simple Medicare expansion would yield savings is by reducing the ability of hospital monopolies to overcharge private insurers. Medicare, in contrast, is able to pay 22 percent less for the same services because of its size. If all Americans used Medicare savings on hospital costs could exceed $53 billion.

These three areas then would save just under $220 billion, bringing the cost down to $618 billion.

One Small Step

While $618 billion still seems like a hefty price tag, taxes wouldn't have to be raised much to pay for it.

For starters, most everyone would pay the premiums already charged by Medicare. This would generate an additional $210 billion in revenue from premiums.

In addition, a Medicare expansion would reduce the need for two current insurance subsidies: one for employer-provided insurance plans and another that the ACA provides insurers. This would save about $161 billion.

This leaves about $246 billion that would still need to be raised through additional taxes. This could be done with an increase in the Medicare tax that gets deducted from your paycheck. The tax, which is split evenly between employee and employer, would need to rise to 5.9 percent from 2.9 percent today. This would amount to just under $15 a week for the typical employee.

Campaigns for universal health insurance coverage have failed in the United States when they run up against the cost of providing coverage. Medicare, America's greatest success in advancing health care, succeeded precisely because it was limited and had its own dedicated funding streams.

We might learn from this example. Rather than jump all the way to a comprehensive single-payer system like the one Sanders favors, we could take a step along the way at a fraction of the cost by simply expanding Medicare to everyone who wants it.

> *"How can we create a society where people aren't so worried about getting old, where there's less stereotyping of older people, more inter-generational contact, and more opportunities to see older people as assets?"*

It's Time to Appreciate Older Workers

Sarah Johnson

In the following viewpoint Sarah Johnson argues that society should not be so quick to write off baby boomers and their potential contributions to the workforce. The author laments the tendency of some in society to show a lack of appreciation to what the most experienced workers can bring to the workplace. She expresses an understanding that older people feel a need and desire to be useful and remain viable cogs in businesses in which many have worked for decades. Johnson understands that Father Time is unbeaten, but she encourages readers to maintain an open mind about baby boomers and the valuable skills they bring to the labor force. Sarah Johnson is a commissioning editor and writer at the Guardian.

"How Can Older People Play A Bigger Role in Society?" by Sarah Johnson, Guardian News and Media Limited, March 30, 2015. Reprinted by permission.

As you read, consider the following questions:

1. Why does Sarah Johnson fear that aging baby boomers will be underappreciated and underutilized by American society?
2. What benefits does the author feel older people can bring to youth in the future?
3. Do you believe that those interviewed for this viewpoint have an agenda to promote the elderly as more useful than generally perceived?

Society is failing to value and harness older people's skills, knowledge and experience, a Guardian survey has revealed. Some 92% of the 1,250 respondents to the ageing population research believe that older adults' contribution to society is not recognised.

One said: "On the whole the public view older people as a drain on society instead of an asset." Another added: "Older people are mostly seen as a bundle of problems and service-needs. Their strengths, skills and knowledge are not harnessed or appreciated in a society infatuated by the cult of youth."

In fact, older people in the UK contribute an estimated £61bn to the economy through employment, volunteering and caring. And, according to Ros Altmann, the UK government's champion for older workers, being 50, 60 or 70 in the 21st century is no longer a predictor of physical or mental abilities. It certainly does not signify that someone has failing health and will soon be unfit to work, or no longer able to learn new skills.

Meanwhile, with numbers of people aged 75 and over expected to double by 2040 and the proportion of older people in the UK due to rise from 23% to 28% of the population by 2030, it is vital to plan for the necessary services to support our ageing society.

How can we create a society where people aren't so worried about getting old, where there's less stereotyping of older people, more inter-generational contact, and more opportunities to see older people as assets? What are the issues around financing retirement and how do we make sure older adults are not excluded because they don't have enough money?

What Do People Worry About as They Grow Older?

Anna McEwen, director of support and development, Shared Lives Plus: Older people have different expectations these days, and that will continue to change. What might have been good enough for previous generations will not cut it in the future, and what we have is not sustainable anyway. I certainly don't want to end up in a care home, nor do I want to have to make the decision for my parents to go into one. I have worked with many older people who have just wanted to stay in their own homes. It's about choice, having the services in place to support people to make choices about how they want to live, and be supported when necessary in later life.

Gemma Heath, PA Consulting Group: I think broadly the things people worry about are the same throughout life—finances, wellbeing, loneliness etc—but as people get older their feeling of being able to control these things changes.

Roger Newman, older person and LGBT activist: My concerns are the usual things like health, mortality, money, etc, but having a feeling of significance is also important.

Are There Stereotypes of Older People?

McEwen: Yes there are. Intergenerational work is a great way to break down barriers between groups of people. For young people to appreciate the experiences and skills of older people and vice versa so that we foster greater understanding between groups of people.

Helen Creighton and George Holley-Moore, International Longevity Centre: There are certainly stereotypes surrounding the baby boomers—well off retirees who maybe took early retirement, own a couple of properties and take frequent holidays. While we have made significant strides in reducing pensioner poverty in the last 20 years (previously to be old meant most likely you would be poor), there is still a significant number of older people living in

BABY BOOMERS WILL DRIVE THE HEALTH TECHNOLOGY OF TOMORROW

When most people envision the health tech of tomorrow, they imagine shiny new handheld devices and health trackers sported by young, healthy adults in their prime.

The truth is that healthcare innovations are generally driven by the population most in need of care...Baby Boomers. Not only do older Americans consume an outsize proportion of healthcare, but they also have a well-funded and effective lobbying infrastructure in support of their needs.

But Boomers are not waiting around for someone to program the clock on their VCR. Defined as those born between 1946 and 1964, they have very different attitudes about aging than their parents did. They want to live active, participatory lives, even as they get older. This segment of the population also has a track record of embracing innovation. They were among the early adopters of devices like personal computers and cellphones that now are commonplace but once were considered groundbreaking.

This then is an engaged, motivated group committed to managing their care in support of a healthier lifestyle through technology. Consider

poverty today. And with wealth inequality comes health inequality, as the Marmot report of 2010 pointed out.

Gillian Connor, head of external affairs, Hanover: I think that older age is still seen as a shorthand for ill-health, inactivity and decline and therefore that stereotype can prevail. There is also an unhelpful stereotype of older people as being anti-youth. There is such brilliant diversity in older age now—you really can't generalise about a group who may range from 50 to 100+.

What Role Do Older People Play in Society at the Moment?

McEwen: Older people have a wealth of skills and experiences, they have lived through situations others cannot even imagine, and yet we continue to dismiss these lifetimes of experiences when that in 2000, only 14% of adults 65 or older were online. By 2016, that percentage had jumped to 64%. Older Americans like using digital technology for the same reasons that others do: to learn, to keep in touch with others, to simplify tasks. In many ways, our future is in very capable hands as the technology younger Americans come to embrace later in life will already be battle tested.

When it comes to health related technology, indicators say that significant numbers of older Americans already are willing to use wearables and other technology to keep track of their health and fitness. An Accenture survey shows that 17% of Americans 65 and over are using the devices, only slightly behind the 20% of Americans under 65 using them. And those that aren't doing so already are willing to start using them: 48% of those 65+ vs. 47% under 65.

Much of this interest is driven by the fact that Boomers have different ideas about what aging should look like versus the generation that preceded them. They want to stay active and abhor the idea of ending up in a nursing home; most desire to remain in their own homes as long as possible.

"Why Baby Boomers Will Drive the Health Technology of Tomorrow," by Paul Oran, Becker's Healthcare, May 22, 2017.

they begin to need care and support and instead people become a list of care needs.

Heath: Older people contribute on a macro level to the workplace and financially and at a local level to their communities and individual networks in terms of experience. They have also contributed for many decades which is something which is often forgotten.

Creighton and Moore: Recent research by the ILC estimated that workers over the age of 50 contribute €2.5tr to the Eurozone economy every year, and many older people also contribute to the economy informally—by caring for their grandchildren or other family members. Figures from the Family and Childcare trust report that 2.3 million grandparents say that they look after their grandchildren in order to enable the children's parents to go to work.

How Is the Environment Geared Towards (Or Against) Older People Taking Part in Their Communities?

Simon Bottery, director of policy and external relations, Independent Age: There are so many simple things that could be improved. For example, most people over 65 walk more slowly than the 1.2 metres per second that is assumed at pedestrian crossings. The result is older people rushing to get across a road as the lights turn to green and the traffic begins to move.

Newman: In Singapore the elderly have smart cards that they can swipe at road crossings and thus slow down the speed that traffic lights change.

Heath: I would extend the "environment" to include people's homes. How are we ensuring that people's homes are adequate for them to remain independent and happy in? Local authorities should review their funding policies to ensure home solutions such as telecare and assistive technology are free to all with substantial need. This supports a reduction in demand on other healthcare services for example A&E departments when issues arise.

Connor: Small things, like well-placed benches for people to rest if they can't walk so well, public toilet provision and thoughtful use of lighting and colour to aid those with dementia can be the difference between being active and housebound.

Creighton and Moore: Making active transport (walking, cycling) more accessible for older people is important. In the UK, cycling remains a disproportionately young (and male) mode of transport. In the Netherlands and Germany, for example, it is far more common for older people to cycle. Improving cycle routes to make them safer is a start. In Scandinavia, planning laws encourage mixed-use development, making journeys from the home to shops and services a lot shorter, and more accessible for older people.

This has obvious health benefits, but also can reduce isolation in our older population.

Anthea Tinker, professor of social gerontology, King's College London: The Age Friendly City research in London showed that there were some excellent features such as the freedom pass and better accessibility on buses and tubes but some way to go with such things as overcrowding, antisocial behaviour, lack of handrails and not enough time to cross roads at traffic lights.

What Employment Opportunities Are There for Older People?

Newman: I chair a local medical centre patient participation group and we have a number of older members who are using their skills in the workplace. However, working in later life needs to acknowledge our need for flexibility especially when our staying power might be reduced. Job sharing and part-time work can be ideal for us.

Jonathan Morgan, senior service manager, Red Cross independent living services in London: There are a number of opportunities to increase work opportunities for older people, someone mentioned previously that the third sector has notoriously low numbers of older people as employees despite having the most experience of advocating for them as a group. It's a cultural shift that's needed so that young people growing up are understanding the value of older people and the many benefits they can bring to the workplace.

Tinker: There is evidence of age discrimination in the workplace as the recent government report A New Vision for Older Workers: Retain, Retrain Recruit shows.

Interestingly more older people are becoming self employed.

> *"A majority of today's employees*
> *expect to work beyond the*
> *traditional retirement age of 65,*
> *with some projecting that they might*
> *never retire."*

An Aging Workforce Highlights the Need for Flexibility

Marcie Pitt-Catsouphes

In the following viewpoint Marcie Pitt-Catsouphes argues that American workers are increasingly projected to work long past the traditional retirement age. If that is the case, the author contends, then it is up to employers to accommodate them. Employers should consider alternative schedules, flexibility in workload, and ability to work remotely. The author notes that this trend is not likely to change as future generations age, so employers should figure it out now. Marcie Pitt-Catsouphes is professor of social work at Boston College.

As you read, consider the following questions:

1. By 2022, what percentage of the US labor force will be aged 55 and older?
2. What two factors have made work more flexible compared to the 1980s?
3. What are some examples of flexibility that workers of the future may enjoy?

There are two quiet trends that might very well transform the structure of work in the near future.

First, a majority of today's employees expect to work beyond the traditional retirement age of 65, with some projecting that they might never retire. In fact, workers aged 55 and older will make up about one-quarter of the US workforce by 2022, according to a US Bureau of Labor Statistics forecast.

Clearly, it is in employers' self-interest to ensure that these employees are as productive and engaged as possible. Employers searching for ways to bolster employee engagement often find that flexible work options—whether in terms of schedules, reduced hours, remote working or some combination—contribute to their dedication and commitment.

Secondly, most employees aged 50 and older would prefer to have access to some type of alternative schedule, reduced hours arrangement or possibly project-based work that allows them to cycle in and out on a project or consulting basis. While there are many different definitions of workplace flexibility, it is generally understood to refer to policies that allow employees and their supervisors some choice about when, where and the number of hours an employee works.

Fearing Unintended Consequences

Of course, the conversation about workplace flexibility has been going on for a long time. Despite employees' need for and their widespread interest in flexible work options, managers periodically express concerns that such arrangements might result in unintended negative consequences. Surveys of employers have found that some human resource managers continue to worry that their employees might abuse these policies. Sometimes, they anticipate repercussions if they approve one employee's request to use a flexible work option but cannot approve this for another worker. Researchers have reported that some managers worry that it is "more work" to supervise employees working on a flexible arrangement, and others question whether service to customers and clients might be affected.

In the 1980s, when the number of women entering (and re-entering) the workforce dramatically increased, deliberations about flexible work options started to emerge at the workplace. At the time, this innovation seemed downright radical to some supervisors. While many human resources managers understood that the standard 9 to 5, Monday to Friday workday was a legacy of the industrial era, there was still a pervasive, taken-for-granted assumption that most employees (other than those on specific shifts that might require evening and night hours) would conform to this norm. Managers soon found, however, that inflexible work structures were often a mismatch for the "new" workforce.

Aging Workforce Highlights Need for Flexibility

The aging of the workforce has once again focused attention on the need for a fresh look at flexible work options. Study after study finds that today's workers (younger workers as well as older workers) seek flexible work options and hope for a gradual transition to retirement rather than an abrupt labor force withdrawal. In 2014, Transamerica Center for Retirement Studies found that nearly two-thirds of workers aged 16 to 64 have a preference for a gradual transition to retirement. Only 22% expect they will stop working abruptly when they reach retirement age. Interestingly, these findings were similar for employees in all three generations: Baby Boomers, Generation X and Millennials.

The business landscape that surrounds workplace flexibility has changed significantly since the 1980s, with two factors having exploded the relevance of rigid work structures: the global economy and technology. Even many small businesses have suppliers, customers or both in other time zones. And, of course, technology has made it possible for many people to work from remote locations (at least some of the time).

Policy makers in countries around the world also find themselves at a type of crossroads with regard to the extended labor force participation of older adults. Public pension schemes are starting to feel the strain of the retirement of the large segment of older adults. Extended labor force participation can help ease the pressure on social insurance since some people who continue to work for pay will postpone accessing their public pensions.

Some Progress but a Long Way to Go

As a consequence, public leaders, such as Ros Altmann, who is the business champion for older workers in the UK, have started to identify innovations like flexible work options that will expand opportunities for older workers to remain in the workforce longer.

To be sure, there has been some progress since the 1980s. A 2014 survey of US firms with 50 or more employees conducted by the Families and Work Institute in New York found that four of every five employers report that they allow at least some groups of employees to periodically change their starting and quitting times. But less than one-third give this option to most or all of their employees.

Unfortunately, fewer than one in every nine US employers reports that he or she has options that support gradual transitions into complete retirement characterized by labor force withdrawal.

Older workers' interest in workplace flexibility seems like a small ask, but it could make a big difference.

> "Decades of the 1% siphoning off
> America's productivity gains have
> left many or most Boomers in weak
> condition for retirement, while
> medical science gives them longer
> lives. It's a relatively easily solved
> problem given the nation's vast
> wealth and income, as shown by the
> experience of our European peers."

Boomers Are Poorly Prepared for Retirement

Larry Kummer

In the following viewpoint Larry Kummer argues that the United States is unprepared to address the consequences of the impact that baby boomers' retirement will have on the nation. The author cites two reports that paint a bleak future for baby boomers, who are retiring with low savings, large debts, and long life expectancies. Larry Kummer has 37 years of experience in the finance industry in a variety of roles. He is editor of Fabius Maximus.

As you read, consider the following questions:

1. What type of debt do baby boomers have today that previous generations did not at that age?
2. What percentage of households age 65 and older depend on Social Security for most of their income?
3. How can employees and policymakers help turn the bleak projections around?

"Demography is destiny."

— From *The Real Majority* by Richard Scammon and Ben Wattenberg (1970).

"Rising mortgage debt is threatening the retirement security of millions of older Americans. In general, older consumers are carrying more debt, including mortgage, credit card, and even student loan debt, into their retirement years than in previous decades."

— "Snapshot of older consumers and mortgage debt" by the US Consumer Finance Protection Bureau, May 2014.

The rise of the Boomers brought massive and largely unexpected changes to American society. The tsunami of politically active young people revitalized both parties, tilting them to their respective extremes. Their buying of home boosted real estate prices. Their increased productivity with age boosted US growth.

Now most of those trends will flip into reverse during the next few decades. Oddly, despite the intense study of the Age Wave, many important and likely trends have received too-little attention. Such as the coming bust in consumer spending and rise of bankruptcies—as large numbers of Boomers retire with little savings, small or no pensions (other than social security), and large debt levels—facing multi-decade long retirements.

I and others have warned about this, but recently major reports have begun to highlight the danger.

We have a new report by the New York Fed (https://www. newyorkfed.org/newsevents/news/research/2016/rp160212). Here is a Dow Jones News story about it (http://m.nasdaq.com/article/ new-york-fed-finds-large-increase-in-debts-held-by-those-over-age-50-20160212-00427). I'll report more as the Fed releases details.

> Americans in their 50s, 60s and 70s are carrying unprecedented amounts of debt, a shift that reflects both the aging of the baby boomer generation and their greater likelihood of retaining mortgage, auto and student debt at much later ages than previous generations. The average 65-year-old borrower has 47% more mortgage debt and 29% more auto debt than 65-year-olds had in 2003, according to data from the Federal Reserve Bank of New York released Friday. Just over a decade ago, student debt was unheard of among 65-year-olds. Today it is a growing debt category, though it remains smaller for them than autos, credit cards and mortgages.

Also see this major report by the US General Accountability Office (GAO): "Most Households Approaching Retirement Have Low Savings," 12 May 2015 (https://www.gao.gov/products/GAO-15-419)—Summary...

> Many retirees and workers approaching retirement have limited financial resources.
>
> About half of households age 55 and older have no retirement savings (such as in a 401(k) plan or an IRA). According to GAO's analysis of the 2013 Survey of Consumer Finances, many older households without retirement savings have few other resources, such as a defined benefit (DB) plan or nonretirement savings, to draw on in retirement. For example, among households age 55 and older, about 29% have neither retirement savings nor a DB plan, which typically provides a monthly payment for life.
>
> Households that have retirement savings generally have other resources to draw on, such as non-retirement savings

and DB plans. Among those with some retirement savings, the median amount of those savings is about $104,000 for households age 55-64 and $148,000 for households age 65-74, equivalent to an inflation-protected annuity of $310 and $649 per month, respectively.

Social Security provides most of the income for about half of households age 65 and older.

… As baby boomers move into retirement each year, the Census Bureau projects that the age 65-and-older population will grow over 50% between 2015 and 2030. Several issues call attention to the retirement security of this sizeable population, including a shift in private-sector pension coverage from defined benefit plans to defined contribution plans, longer life expectancies, and uncertainty about Social Security's long-term financial condition. In light of these developments, GAO was asked to review the financial status of workers approaching retirement and of current retirees.

Expect to See More Articles About Folly of the Poor

How sad that the poor spend their savings to live, as described in "Nearly Half of U.S. Employees Cash Out Their 401(k) Accounts When Leaving Their Jobs," Hewitt Associates, 28 October 2009. They worry about the lack of discipline and foresight among the lower classes and young people. Pamela Hess, Hewitt's director of retirement research, explains…

> Particularly during the economic downturn, employers and financial advisors have been increasingly vocal about the negative impact that cashing out of a 401(k) plan has on retirement savings. But employees don't seem to be getting the message. In a society where less than 1 in 5 workers will likely be able to meet their needs in retirement, employers and policymakers need to work together to implement solutions that change employee behaviors and reduce cash-out rates. Otherwise, millions of Americans who rely on defined contribution plans will find themselves unable to achieve a financially secure retirement.

What wonderful advice for the unemployed: give up eating and go live under a bridge. These are the keys to a secure retirement. Nowhere in this does it suggest that the unemployed might need to spend their retirement money in order to survive now.

Conclusions

Decades of the 1% siphoning off America's productivity gains have left many or most Boomers in weak condition for retirement, while medical science gives them longer lives. It's a relatively easily solved problem given the nation's vast wealth and income, as shown by the experience of our European peers.

What can we expect? Boomers become sellers of their assets, largely homes and stocks—with a depressing effect on their prices. Retiring boomers slashing discretionary consumption—a strong drag on the vendors of those goods and services, and on the overall US economy. A rising rate of bankruptcies.

Unless we take large-scale public policy action, these effects are baked in, as usual for demographic trends on the one and two decade time-frame.

> *"Yes, this means exactly what you think it does: Millennials might actually be doing something good for the sustainability of our future."*

Maybe a Declining Birth Rate Isn't All Bad

Meghan McNamara

In the following viewpoint, Meghan McNamara argues that perhaps we don't need to worry about the consequences of the dramatic differences between the aging baby boomer and the emerging millennial generations. The author points to factors that worry politicians and economists, such as a declining birth rate and changes in the labor force due to the aging baby boomers. She contends that a lower birth rate is actually healthier for the planet, and the workforce will be altered anyway by factors such as automation. The author suggests that the country will simply need to adapt to the differences in new generations and that one is not better than another. Megan McNamara is a writer and founding editor of Stillhouse Press.

"Millennials: It's OK, Baby Boomers," by Meghan McNamara, Medium, February 6, 2019. https://medium.com/@meghanmcnamara/its-ok-baby-boomers-f8b5463d240f Licensed under CC BY-ND 4.0 International.

As you read, consider the following questions:

1. What drop in the general fertility rate was considered a 30-year record low according to the viewpoint?
2. How may automation of labor factor into millennials' lower birth rate according to the author?
3. How can a declining birth rate help the environment according to the viewpoint?

We have been hearing it for the better part of a decade now: The national birth rate is falling and it's a total doomsday scenario.

The Centers for Disease Control released its National Vital Statistics report in early January and, for the third year in a row, the general fertility rate (GFR) has dropped again. According to the report, the GFR has decreased 3 percent since 2016, hitting a 30-year record low.

It's the millennials. [Insert blame here].

We are nothing like our parents. We change jobs more frequently—often several times during our most productive working lives—marry later, and don't save for retirement like we should.

Our culture and our environment are nothing like our baby boomer parents' either. We came of age in an often unstable gig economy (I graduated from college in 2008, at the height of the economic crisis), much of our mate finding is now the product of online matchmaking; and millennials have some of the most staggering levels of student loan debt. And, to make matters even more concerning, infant and mother mortality rates have been consistently on the rise, making the United States among one of the most dangerous places to give birth in the industrialized world (not to mention one of the most expensive).

So yes, there is plenty of evidence to support why millennials are not having as many children, but the larger question is not so much how do we change this, but rather: Is the diminishing birthrate really such a bad thing?

Maybe We Really Are Worried About Becoming Our Parents

First, let's address the unease about our aging workforce, which has been proposed as one of the primary apprehensions of the falling birthrate. For those who make this argument, I would point to this Nov. 2018 article (https://www.newsweek.com/2018/11/30/ai-and-automation-will-replace-most-human-workers-because-they-dont-have-be-1225552.html)—one of many released since the early aughts—which suggests we should also be concerned about how automated our workforce is becoming.

In truth, automation is most a threat to low-skilled, blue collar jobs, which are more compulsory in an economy that fails to incentivize education and technical job skills, instead spurring children of low wage earners to follow in their parents footsteps.

But if colleges and technical schools were made more affordable, forthcoming generations might actually have the opportunity to learn skills and trades their parents were never afforded the opportunity to, consequently paving the way for manual labor jobs to become more mechanized.

It's a crazy notion, I know. But when did we stop wanting our children to have better lives than our own?

I have a distinct memory of discussing my plans for college with my father, who received not one, but two Bachelors degrees. "All I want," I recall my father saying, "is for my children to be smarter and more educated than I am."

He did not live long enough to see this wish come true, though it did eventually come to fruition. (In 2016, I received my Master of Fine Arts in Creative Writing and a whopping five-digit student loan bill to pair with it.)

I digress.

While I'm all for a more socialized form of education, that's not my primary argument here. Rather, I would suggest this downward trend of childrearing is actually a very good thing, not just domestically, but from a global perspective as well.

We're Not Just Poor and Childless; We Also Love the Planet

As a millennial, a childfree woman, and an environmental steward, I have profound concerns about the future of the world as we know it—especially given the current trajectory of the U.S., where we have done little to limit carbon dioxide emissions, despite daunting predictions from the environmental community about our warming world and the growing occurrence of climate-related disasters.

And I'm not alone. According to a July 2018 New York Times survey of nearly 2,000 men and women ages 20 to 45, 33 percent of respondents cited worries about climate change as a reason for having fewer children than they had expected to or considered ideal.

In recent years, catastrophic weather events have increased dramatically, and with CO_2 emissions still on the rise, world food shortages and shrinking coastlines are becoming less prediction and more reality. According to analyses conducted annually by the World Bank, in order to reach climate targets and avoid severe global warming, we must reduce carbon emissions in the United States by two tonnes per person, per year by 2050—a considerable reduction, given that the average U.S. citizen produces just more than 16 tonnes of carbon per person, per year (as of 2019, that number is estimated to have reached roughly 20 tonnes per person, per year).

Some of the most substantial ways to reduce emissions, according to a 2017 Environmental Research Letters study, include eating a plant-based diet, reducing air travel, living car-free, and—perhaps the most significant impact by a long mile—having one fewer child.

It's also worth noting that most major analyses for reducing emissions (and remaining under the 2°C point-of-no-return benchmark that the Intergovernmental Panel on Climate Change has established) assumes the use of unproven technologies to achieve emissions cuts. Thus, in order to truly make an impact, it's ever more important we consider real life applications, which we can begin making now.

Yes, this means exactly what you think it does: Millennials might actually be doing something good for the sustainability of our future.

Just ask Edward S. Rubenstein, president of ESR Research and an experienced researcher, financial analyst, and economics journalist. While most economists agree that a declining birthrate spells trouble for the growth of Gross Domestic Product (GDP), Rubin concludes that it might actually be very good for our environment, specifically as it relates to scarcity of resources and the earth's natural ability to replenish these resources.

Go ahead, let's all take a collective sigh of relief.

Rubenstein concludes that millennials "seem determined to break away from the spendthrift, materialistic ways of their baby boomer parents," the longterm benefits of which could mean "a lower U.S. population, a lower per capita carbon footprint, [and] the proliferation of renewable energy sources."

In other words, our very decision not to have children at quite the same rate as previous generations, might be the very thing that ensures the children we do choose to have actually inhabit a livable world. Wild, I know.

And so I say (tongue firmly inserted into cheek): Watch out, baby boomers. We may just be your only hope.

Periodical and Internet Sources Bibliography

The following articles have been selected to supplement the diverse views presented in this chapter.

Toni Blumberg, "70% of Americans Now Support Medicare-for-All —Here's How Single-Payer Can Affect You," Make It, August 28, 2018. https://www.cnbc.com/2018/08/28/most-americans-now-support-medicare-for-all-and-free-college-tuition.html.

Paul Davidson, "Older Workers Are Driving Job Growth as Boomers Remain in Workforce Longer," *USA Today*, January 9, 2019. https://www.usatoday.com/story/money/2019/01/09/boomers-older-workers-work-longer-driving-job-growth/2496893002/.

Dona DeZube, "Bye Bye Boomers: Who Will Fill Your Workforce Gap?" Monster. https://hiring.monster.com/employer-resources/recruiting-strategies/workforce-planning/baby-boomer-workforce-gap/.

Adinah East, "Baby Boomers in an Aging Population: How Our Healthcare System Will Be Forever Changed," Caring People, January 2, 2018. https://caringpeopleinc.com/blog/baby-boomers-aging-population/.

Justin Fox, "The Long Baby Boomer Reign Isn't Ending Just Yet," Bloomberg, April 29, 2018. https://www.bloomberg.com/opinion/articles/2018-04-29/long-reign-of-the-baby-boomers-isn-t-over.

Eva Kohana and Boaz Kohana, "Baby Boomers' Expectations of Health and Medicine," *AMA Journal of Ethics*, May 2014. https://journalofethics.ama-assn.org/article/baby-boomers-expectations-health-and-medicine/2014-05.

Bailey Nelson, "How to Get the Best Out of Baby Boomers," Gallup, February 5, 2019. https://www.gallup.com/workplace/246443/best-baby-boomers.aspx.

Laura Schneider, "The Impact of the Aging Workforce on the Technology Industry," The Balance Careers, January 17, 2019. https://www.thebalancecareers.com/retiring-boomers-affect-job-market-2071932.

OPPOSING
VIEWPOINTS®
SERIES

CHAPTER 3

Does a Growing Population Create a Growing Problem?

Chapter Preface

The date was October 17, 2016. The time was 7:46 a.m. At that moment the population of the United States reached 300 million. It had surpassed 200 million only forty-nine years earlier and 100 million fifty-two years previous during the height of European immigration.

Though the birth rate had slowed by the second decade of the twenty-first century—it was reported in 2018 that more Americans were dying than being born—the sheer number of people inhabiting the land will result in an epic responsibility for society in the present through the distant future. Does the nation boast enough resources to take care of everyone? Will income inequality become so pervasive that the rich will actually become richer and the poor become poorer in a country with already the largest disparity in the world?

The issues of population growth are spotlighted in the following chapter. So are related problems, such as the effect of immigration and competition for college educations that have resulted in numbing student debt. Upticks in immigration while at the same time decreases in the white population mean that more than 50 percent of Americas will be non-white by the middle of the century, according to projections. Meanwhile, young people are entering their twenties significantly behind their parents economically, the result of maddeningly exorbitant tuition and housing costs that place them tens of thousands of dollars in the hole by the time they graduate. It is no wonder politicians have called for free tuition for American students. But how will funding such an ambitious plan affect the economy?

Concerns about population growth have vexed the American people and their leaders for generations. It remains to be seen if the problems it causes will be solved or worsened by future ideas and policies.

> "Overall, a majority of Americans have positive views about immigrants. Six-in-ten Americans (65%) say immigrants strengthen the country 'because of their hard work and talents,' while just over a quarter (26%) say immigrants burden the country by taking jobs, housing and health care."

Do Immigrants Add Value to America?

Gustavo López, Kristen Bialik, and Jynnah Radford

In the following viewpoint Jynnah Radford uses statistics to examine the state of the US immigrant population. The issue of immigration was placed front and center as arguably the most controversial topic during the 2016 presidential campaign and the early years of Donald Trump's presidency. The data in this viewpoint serves to set the record straight about the number of immigrants entering the country, how they affect population growth, the number that enter illegally, their motivations, and the nations from which they come. In an era of heated arguments that often include misinformation about immigration, such articles prove valuable by providing truthful statistics. The authors are researchers at Pew Research Center.

"Key Findings About U.S. Immigrants," by Gustavo López, Kristen Bialik and Jynnah Radford, Pew Research Center, Washington, DC (November 30, 2018). http://www. pewresearch.org/fact-tank/2018/11/30/key-findings-about-u-s-immigrants/. Used in accordance with Pew Research Center reuse Policy. http://www.pewresearch.org/terms-and-conditions/. Usage in no way implies endorsement.

As you read, consider the following questions:

1. Can a point of view be deduced from this statistically dominated article?
2. What do you believe is the most important finding in this listing of information about immigration?
3. Why has the distinction between legal and illegal immigration become such a flashpoint for debate?

The United States has more immigrants than any other country in the world. Today, more than 40 million people living in the US were born in another country, accounting for about one-fifth of the world's migrants in 2016. The population of immigrants is also very diverse, with just about every country in the world represented among U.S. immigrants.

Pew Research Center regularly publishes statistical portraits of the nation's foreign-born population, which include historical trends since 1960. Based on these portraits, here are answers to some key questions about the U.S. immigrant population.

How Many People in the U.S. Are Immigrants?

The U.S. foreign-born population reached a record 43.7 million in 2016. Since 1965, when U.S. immigration laws replaced a national quota system, the number of immigrants living in the U.S. has more than quadrupled. Immigrants today account for 13.5% of the U.S. population, nearly triple the share (4.7%) in 1970. However, today's immigrant share remains below the record 14.8% share in 1890, when 9.2 million immigrants lived in the U.S.

What Is the Legal Status of Immigrants in the U.S.?

Most immigrants (76%) are in the country legally, while a quarter are unauthorized, according to new Pew Research Center estimates based on census data adjusted for undercount. In 2016, 45% were naturalized U.S. citizens.

Some 27% of immigrants were permanent residents and 5% were temporary residents in 2016. Another 24% of all immigrants were unauthorized immigrants. From 1990 to 2007, the unauthorized immigrant population tripled in size—from 3.5 million to a record high of 12.2 million. During the Great Recession, the number declined by 1 million and since then has leveled off. In 2016, there were 10.7 million unauthorized immigrants in the U.S., accounting for 3.3% of the nation's population.

The decline in the unauthorized immigrant population is due largely to a fall in the number from Mexico—the single largest group of unauthorized immigrants in the U.S. Between 2007 and 2016, this group decreased by more than 1 million. Meanwhile, there was a rise in the number from Central America.

Do All Lawful Immigrants Choose to Become U.S. Citizens?

Not all lawful permanent residents choose to pursue U.S. citizenship. Those who wish to do so may apply after meeting certain requirements, including having lived in the U.S. for five years. In fiscal year 2017, 986,851 immigrants applied for naturalization. The number of naturalization applications has climbed in recent years, though the annual totals remain below the 1.4 million applications filed in 2007.

Generally, most immigrants eligible for naturalization apply to become citizens. However, Mexican lawful immigrants have the lowest naturalization rate overall. Language and personal barriers, lack of interest and financial barriers are among the top reasons for choosing not to naturalize cited by Mexican-born green card holders, according to a 2015 Pew Research Center survey.

Where Do Immigrants Come From?

Mexico is the top origin country of the U.S. immigrant population. In 2016, 11.6 million immigrants living in the U.S. were from there, accounting for 26% of all U.S. immigrants. The next largest origin groups were those from China (6%), India (6%), the Philippines (4%) and El Salvador (3%).

By region of birth, immigrants from South and East Asia combined accounted for 27% of all immigrants, a share equal to that of Mexico. Other regions make up smaller shares: Europe/Canada (13%), the Caribbean (10%), Central America (8%), South America (7%), the Middle East (4%) and sub-Saharan Africa (4%).

Who Is Arriving Today?

More than 1 million immigrants arrive in the U.S. each year. In 2016, the top country of origin for new immigrants coming into the U.S. was India, with 126,000 people, followed by Mexico (124,000), China (121,000) and Cuba (41,000).

By race and ethnicity, more Asian immigrants than Hispanic immigrants have arrived in the U.S. each year since 2010. Immigration from Latin America slowed following the Great Recession, particularly from Mexico, which has seen net decreases in U.S. immigration over the past few years.

Asians are projected to become the largest immigrant group in the U.S. by 2055, surpassing Hispanics. Pew Research Center estimates indicate that in 2065, Asians will make up some 38% of all immigrants; Hispanics, 31%; whites, 20%; and blacks, 9%.

Is the Immigrant Population Growing?

New immigrant arrivals have fallen, mainly due to a decrease in the number of unauthorized immigrants coming to the U.S. The fall in the growth of the unauthorized immigrant population can partly be attributed to more Mexican immigrants leaving the U.S. than coming in.

Looking forward, immigrants and their descendants are projected to account for 88% U.S. population growth through 2065, assuming current immigration trends continue. In addition to new arrivals, U.S. births to immigrant parents will be important to future U.S. growth. In 2016, the percentage of women giving birth in the past year was higher among immigrants (7.4%) than among the U.S. born (5.9%). While U.S.-born women gave birth to over 3 million children that year, immigrant women gave birth to more than 750,000.

How Many Immigrants Have Come to the U.S. as Refugees?

Since the creation of the federal Refugee Resettlement Program in 1980, about 3 million refugees have been resettled in the U.S—more than any other country.

In fiscal 2017, a total of 53,716 refugees were resettled in the U.S. The largest origin group of refugees was the Democratic Republic of the Congo, followed by Iraq, Syria, Somalia, and Burma (Myanmar). Among all refugees admitted in that fiscal year, 22,861 are Muslims (43%) and 25,194 are Christians (47%). California, Texas and New York resettled nearly a quarter of all refugees admitted in fiscal 2016.

Where Do Most U.S. Immigrants Live?

Roughly half (46%) of the nation's 43.7 million immigrants live in just three states: California (24%), Texas (11%) and New York (10%). California had the largest immigrant population of any state in 2016, at 10.7 million. Texas and New York had more than 4.5 million immigrants each.

In terms of regions, about two-thirds of immigrants lived in the West (34%) and South (33%). Roughly one-fifth lived in the Northeast (21%) and 11% were in the Midwest.

In 2016, most immigrants lived in just 20 major metropolitan areas, with the largest populations in New York, Los Angeles and Miami. These top 20 metro areas were home to 28.3 million immigrants, or 65% of the nation's total. Most of the nation's unauthorized immigrant population lived in these top metro areas as well.

How Do Immigrants Compare with the U.S. Population Overall in Education?

Immigrants in the U.S. as a whole have lower levels of education than the U.S.-born population. In 2016, immigrants were three times as likely as the U.S. born to have not completed high school (29% vs. 9%). However, immigrants were just as likely as the U.S. born to have a college degree or more, 32% and 30% respectively.

Educational attainment varies among the nation's immigrant groups, particularly across immigrants from different regions of the world. Immigrants from Mexico (57%) and Central America (49%) are less likely to be high school graduates than the U.S. born (9%). On the other hand, immigrants from South and East Asia, Europe, Canada, the Middle East and sub-Saharan Africa were more likely than U.S.-born residents to have a bachelor's or advanced degree.

Among all immigrants, those from South and East Asia (52%) and the Middle East (47%) were the most likely to have a bachelor's degree or more. Immigrants from Mexico (6%) and Central America (9%) were the least likely to have a bachelor's or higher.

How Many Immigrants are Working in the U.S.?

In 2016, about 28 million immigrants were working or looking for work in the U.S., making up some 17% of the total civilian labor force. Lawful immigrants made up the majority of the immigrant workforce, at 20.6 million. An additional 7.8 million immigrant workers are unauthorized immigrants, the first time since 2006 that the number was significantly below 8 million. They alone account for 4.8% of the civilian labor force, a dip from their peak of 5.4% in 2007. During the same period, the overall U.S. workforce grew, as did the number of U.S.-born workers and lawful immigrant workers.

Immigrants, regardless of legal status, work in a variety of jobs and do not make up the majority of workers in any U.S. industry. Lawful immigrants are most likely work in professional, management, or business and finance jobs (38%) or service jobs

(21%). Unauthorized immigrants, by contrast, are most likely to be working in service (31%) or construction jobs (17%).

Immigrants are also projected to drive future growth in the U.S. working-age population through at least 2035. As the Baby Boom generation heads into retirement, immigrants and their children are expected to offset a decline in the working-age population by adding about 18 million people of working age between 2015 and 2035.

How Well Do Immigrants Speak English?

Among immigrants ages 5 and older, half (51%) are proficient English speakers—either speaking English very well (35%) or only speaking English at home (16%).

Immigrants from Mexico have the lowest rates of English proficiency (32%), followed by Central Americans (33%) and immigrants from South and East Asia (54%). Those from Europe or Canada (76%), sub-Saharan Africa (72%), and the Middle East (61%) have the highest rates of English proficiency.

The longer immigrants have lived in the U.S., the greater the likelihood they are English proficient. Some 44% of immigrants living in the U.S. five years or less are proficient. By contrast, more than half (55%) of immigrants who have lived in the U.S. for 20 years or more are proficient English speakers.

Among immigrants ages 5 and older, Spanish is the most commonly spoken language. Some 43% of immigrants in the U.S. speak Spanish at home. The top five languages spoken at home among immigrants outside of Spanish are English only (16%), followed by Chinese (6%), Hindi (5%), Filipino/Tagalog (4%) and French (3%).

How Many Immigrants Have Been Deported Recently?

Around 340,000 immigrants were deported from the U.S. in fiscal 2016, slightly up since 2015. Overall, the Obama administration deported about 3 million immigrants between 2009 and 2016,

THE WIDENING WEALTH GAP

The racial and ethnic wealth gap has evolved differently for families at different income levels, according to a Pew Research Center analysis of data from the Federal Reserve Board's Survey of Consumer Finances released Wednesday. "Among lower-income families, the gap between white households and their black and Hispanic counterparts shrank by about half from 2007 to 2016. But among middle-class families, it increased and shows no sign of retreating," it said.

Here are three takeaways:

- Wealth gaps between upper-income families, lower- and middle-income families are at the highest levels recorded
- Last year, the median wealth of white households was 10 times the wealth of black households and eight times that of Hispanic households

- The racial and ethnic wealth gap has evolved differently for families at different income levels

The Great Recession triggered a sharp, prolonged decline in the wealth of American families and, despite the recovery in the housing market and stock market over the last decade, U.S. household wealth has not fully recovered, the research concluded. In 2016, the median wealth of all U.S. households was $97,300, up 16% from

a significantly higher number than the 2 million immigrants deported by the Bush administration between 2001 and 2008.

Immigrants convicted of a crime made up the minority of deportations in 2016, the most recent year for which statistics by criminal status are available. Of the 340,000 immigrants deported in 2016, some 40% had criminal convictions and 60% were not convicted of a crime. From 2001 to 2016, a majority (60%) of immigrants deported have not been convicted of a crime.

2013 but well below median wealth before the recession began in late 2007 ($139,700 in 2016 dollars), Pew found.

White Americans, meanwhile, have overwhelmingly benefited from the rise in incomes, according to a separate report released last month by the Urban Institute, a nonprofit policy group based in Washington, D.C., while most other groups have been left behind. Looking at private income, such as earnings and dividends, and government benefits like Social Security, the income of families near the top increased roughly 90% from 1963 to 2016, while the income of families at the bottom rose less than 10%.

Here are three more takeaways:

- The richest households now have 12 times the wealth of families in the middle of the income spectrum versus 6 times the wealth in 1963
- Those in the middle more than doubled their wealth over the same period while families wealthier than 90% of all households saw their wealth increase fivefold

- At the same time, the poorest 10% families in America went from having no wealth in 1963 to being $1,000 in debt in 2016

Families of color will soon make up a majority of the U.S. population, but most continue to fall behind Caucasians in building wealth.

"7 Charts Explain Why the Gap Between the Rich and Poor Is Highest Ever," by Quentin Fottrell, MarketWatch, Inc, November 4, 2017.

How Many Immigrants Are Apprehended at the U.S.-Mexico Border?

The number of apprehensions at the U.S.-Mexico border has sharply decreased over the past decade or so, from more than 1 million in fiscal 2006 to 303,916 in fiscal 2017. Today, there are more apprehensions of non-Mexicans than Mexicans at the border. In fiscal 2017, apprehensions of Central Americans at the border exceeded those of Mexicans for the third time since 2014.

How Do Americans View Immigrants and Immigration?

While immigration has been at the forefront of a national political debate, the U.S. public holds a range of views about immigrants living in the country. Overall, a majority of Americans have positive views about immigrants. Six-in-ten Americans (65%) say immigrants strengthen the country "because of their hard work and talents," while just over a quarter (26%) say immigrants burden the country by taking jobs, housing and health care.

Yet these views vary starkly by political affiliation. Among Democrats and Democratic-leaning independents, 84% think immigrants strengthen the country with their hard work and talents, and just 12% say they are a burden. Among Republicans and Republican-leaning independents, roughly as many (44%) say immigrants are a burden as say immigrants strengthen the country because of their hard work and talents (42%).

Americans also hold more positive views of some immigrant groups than others, according to a 2015 Pew Research Center immigration report. More than four-in-ten Americans expressed mostly positive views of Asian (47%) and European immigrants (44%), yet only a quarter expressed such views of African and Latin American immigrants (26% each). Roughly half of the U.S. public said immigrants are making things better through food, music and the arts (49%), but almost equal shares said immigrants are making crime and the economy worse (50% each).

Americans were divided on future levels of immigration. Nearly half said immigration to the U.S. should be decreased (49%), while one-third (34%) said immigration should be kept at its present level and just 15% said immigration should be increased.

> "*There can be little doubt that immigrants expand the overall pie; but what about their effect on how that pie is shared? Here the evidence is less clear.*"

Immigration Can Boost the Economy During a Retirement Boom

Jason Furman

In the following viewpoint Jason Furman argues that immigration can result in a much needed boost to the US economy, especially given the high retirement rates experienced in the United States as baby boomers leave the workforce. The author warns, however, that the wave of anti-immigrant sentiment fueled by President Trump and embraced by his supporters hinders growth and creates a higher level of populism and negative nationalism. Jason Furman is Professor of the Practice of Economic Policy at the Harvard Kennedy School and Senior Fellow at the Peterson Institute for International Economics. He was chairman of President Barack Obama's Council of Economic Advisers from 2013 to 2017.

"Nationalism, Immigration, and Economic Success," by Jason Furman, Project Syndicate, July 18, 2018. Reprinted by permission.

As you read, consider the following questions:

1. What arguments does the author give for connecting nationalism with weakened global economies?
2. Why does the author believe immigration can be a boon to the economic health of the United States?
3. What anti-immigrant trend in the early twentieth century does the author cite to make his point?

One of the central challenges facing the world's advanced economies is slowing growth. Over the last decade, growth rates in the advanced economies have averaged 1.2%, down from an average of 3.1% during the previous 25 years.

History shows that slower economic growth can make societies less generous, less tolerant, and less inclusive. So, it stands to reason that the past decade of sluggish growth has contributed to the surge of a damaging form of populist nationalism that is taking hold in a growing number of countries.

As in the darker decades of the 20th century, today's nationalism takes the form of heightened opposition to immigration and—to a lesser degree—free trade. Making matters worse, today's toxic nationalism will exacerbate the economic slowdown that fueled its emergence.

Turning this vicious circle into a virtuous one—in which increased openness drives faster growth—will depend, at least in part, on making immigration more compatible with inclusionary forms of nationalism.

The economic evidence on this issue is clear: immigration makes a strong contribution to economic growth. Moreover, immigration is more necessary than ever, because population aging and lower birthrates across advanced economies are producing a retirement boom without a commensurate cohort of native prime-age workers to support it.

For example, Japan's working-age population has been shrinking since 1995. In the European Union, immigrants accounted for 70%

of labor-force growth from 2000 to 2010. And in the United States, immigration is the primary reason the workforce will continue to grow; if the US relied only on native-born workers, its labor force would shrink.

Faster growth is beneficial even if it must support a larger population, because working immigrants pay taxes that help support pensioners and retirees. In general, it is much better to be a fast-growing country with a vibrant, expanding population than a country with a dwindling population, like Japan.

Moreover, in addition to expanding the workforce, immigrants actually boost per capita gross domestic product by increasing productivity—that is, the amount that each worker produces. The reason is that immigrants are much more likely to be entrepreneurial and to start new businesses.

In Germany, for example, foreign-passport holders started 44% of new businesses in 2015. In France, the Organisation for Economic Co-operation and Development has estimated that immigrants engage in 29% more entrepreneurial activity than native-born workers do, which is similar to the average for the OECD as a whole. And in the US, immigrants take out patents at two to three times the rate of native-born citizens, and their innovations benefit non-immigrants as well.

There can be little doubt that immigrants expand the overall pie; but what about their effect on how that pie is shared? Here the evidence is less clear. There are certainly winners and losers. Yet, on balance, the available evidence suggests that immigrants do not reduce wages for native-born workers. In fact, it is more likely that immigrants increase wages overall.

One recent study of France, for example, found that each 1% increase in immigrants' share of employment within a given département raises its native-born workers' wages by 0.5%. It would seem that in addition to contributing to the size and productivity of the workforce, immigrants also often complement the skills of native-born workers, helping them earn more.

My professional focus is on economics, so I have emphasized the role of growth. But that clearly is not the only factor behind the rise of populist nationalism.

The fact that developed countries are changing culturally also matters, perhaps even more so. In the US, for example, the foreign-born share of the population has risen from 5% in 1960 to around 14% today. As Harvard University's Yascha Mounk notes in his insightful new book, "The People vs. Democracy," that is the highest share since the last major anti-immigrant backlash in the US: the early 20th-century "yellow peril."

The trends are similar, and sometimes even more dramatic, in other developed countries. The foreign-born share of the population in Sweden, for example, has gone from 4% in 1960 to 19% today, representing a much larger shift than that in the US.

All countries face a choice when it comes to immigration. They can pay an economic price to follow a more exclusionary course, or they can reap the economic benefits from greater openness. But while public policies can help ensure that the benefits of openness are realized, we should not lose sight of their political and economic limitations.

Looking beyond policy solutions, we also need to establish a cultural expectation that immigrants will not just bring diverse perspectives, but also join their new country as citizens. That means speaking the language, honoring national traditions, and—as I saw first-hand while discussing these issues at Les Rencontres Économiques in Aix-en-Provence, France—cheering for the national soccer team.

In the US, in particular, that is the vision of immigration and inclusive nationalism that we should be working toward—including the better soccer team.

> "Immigrants have driven two-thirds
> of U.S. economic growth since 2011.
> They founded 30 percent of US firms,
> including more than 50 percent of
> startups valued at over $1 billion."

Immigration Affects the Economy in Positive and Negative Ways

Kimberly Amadeo

In the following viewpoint Kimberly Amadeo argues that millions of documented and undocumented immigrants have assimilated into American society since 1990, after which the number of the latter has tripled and grown to nearly 11 million—3 percent of the total US population. The author provides statistics that offer truth and reason to a heated debate, such as what she believes to be a fallacy perpetrated by President Trump that illegal immigrants commit more crimes than native-born Americans, as well as the motivations of immigrants as asylum seekers. Kimberly Amadeo is the economics and business expert for The Balance and president of WorldMoneyWatch.com.

"Immigration's Effect on the Economy and You," by Kimberly Amadeo, The Balance a part of Dotdash Publishing Family, January 25, 2019. Reprinted by permission.

As you read, consider the following questions:

1. What reasons does the author give for justifying the motivations of undocumented immigrants to cross US borders?
2. Does this viewpoint offer any solutions to the problem of illegal immigration?
3. What view does the author express about the Trump administration's treatment of asylum seekers arriving at the southern border?

In 2016, there were 43.7 million immigrants in the United States. That's 13.5 percent of the total population. About 1 million immigrants a year receive green cards that allow permanent legal resident status.

Immigrants live with 16 million American-born children who are US citizens. Those immigrants and their families make up 25 percent of all US residents. Almost 75 percent are documented immigrants and their children.

Immigrants have less education than the average American. But that's improving. For example, thirty percent of immigrants, 25 and older, lack a high school diploma compared to 9 percent of native-born adults. But that's better than in 1970 when more than half of immigrants lacked a high school diploma.

Furthermore, 30 percent of immigrants have a college degree. That's similar to the 32 percent of native-born counterparts. Forty-seven percent of immigrants who entered between 2012-2016 have that degree.

Undocumented Immigrants

In 2016, there were an estimated 10.7 million undocumented immigrants in the United States. That's 3 percent of the US population of 320 million and 25 percent of the immigrant population. Half of them have lived in the United States for at least 14.8 years.

The number of undocumented immigrants has tripled since 1990, when there were 3.5 million in the United States. But it's down from a peak of 12.2 million in 2007. The recession didn't hit Mexico as hard as it did the United States.

In 2016, there were 7.8 million undocumented immigrants in the workforce. That's down from 8.2 million in 2007. They are mostly in farming and construction.

Almost half or 3.4 million pay Social Security payroll taxes. In 2010, they and their employers contributed $13 billion. They do so even though they are not eligible for Social Security benefits upon retirement. They do this by using outdated Social Security numbers or an Individual Taxpayer Identification Number. They hope that paying taxes will one day help them become a citizen.

The Department of Homeland Security found that 15.5 percent of undocumented immigrants benefit from Medicaid. Around $2 billion a year goes to hospitals who must care for anyone who shows up at the emergency room. It's similar to the 16.1 percent of native-born Americans who use Medicaid. The study found that 9.1 percent of undocumented immigrants used food stamps, compared to 11.6 percent of native-born. Many undocumented immigrants receive the benefits because they live in households with eligible Americans.

Use of welfare is negligible, less than 1 percent, for both populations.

Half are the undocumented immigrants came from Mexico, a little less than the 57 percent in 2007. At the same time, the number from Asia, Africa, and Central America has increased. One reason for the shift is an improvement in Mexico's economy. At the same time, crime in Honduras soared after Salvadoran drug gangs took over. The illegal drug trade to the United States moved there from the Caribbean.

In 2013, the Department of Homeland Security deported a record 434,015 immigrants. The Obama administration deported 2.4 million, and of those, nearly half had a criminal record. It sent home more in its first five years than the Bush administration did in eight years. That's despite deportation relief for 580,946 young immigrants under Obama's Deferred Action for Childhood Arrivals.

There were 1.9 million "removable criminal aliens." That includes both legal and illegal immigrants. President Donald Trump promised to deport them immediately.

Asylum Seekers

In 2016, the US Border Patrol apprehended 415,816 immigrants. US law requires the government to allow anyone who shows up at the border to apply for asylum. They are referred to an asylum officer who determines if they have a "credible fear" of persecution or torture in their home country. Immigrants already in the United States can also apply for asylum to prevent deportation.

In 2015, the government granted asylum to 26,124 applicants. Once immigrants get approved for asylum, they can stay in the United States. They receive authorization to work and apply for a Social Security card. The can apply for Medicaid or Refugee Medical Assistance. They can also petition to bring family members to America.

If the asylum officer doesn't find a credible fear, they order deportation. The refugee can appear before a judge to challenge the finding. In March 2018, there was a backlog of 690,000 deportation cases under review.

Since November 2018, the number of migrant families applying for asylum at the US border has increased. Homeland Security does not have the funding to process the new surge. Many are showing up in remote areas. One reason for the uptick is an increase in drug-related violence. Crime in Honduras soared after Salvadoran drug gangs took over. The illegal drug trade to the United States moved there from the Caribbean.

The goal of Trump's immigration policies is to reduce the number of undocumented immigrants in the country. One reason there are so many undocumented immigrants is that it's so difficult to immigrate with authorization. There are 4 million people on immigration waiting lists. Almost 150 million people who would leave their country if they could and move to the United States.

The Trump administration wants to eliminate the appeals process for asylum seekers. Instead, it wants to criminally charge anyone who shows up at the border without documentation. It also briefly separated children from their parents to discourage other undocumented immigrants.

In November of 2018, the Trump administration vowed to send 5,800 troops to the Mexico border. He sought to defend the US border from a caravan of thousands of Honduran refugees. They were seeking asylum from dangerous conditions in their home country. They banded together to protect each other on the dangerous trek and avoid using human traffickers. In response to this surge, the United States temporarily closed the border to Mexico. Customs agents fired tear gas at members of the caravan who had rushed the border fence.

On December 20, 2018, Trump refused to sign a budget bill because it lacked $5.7 billion to build a wall on the border with Mexico. As a result, nine federal government agencies shut down.

Refugees

In 2015, the US granted 69,920 immigrants refugee status. A refugee applies for protection from persecution while still in their home country. If granted protection, the refugee can live in the United States as long as their home country remains unsafe. They receive a work permit and other government support. After one year, they can apply for a green card. After four years, they can apply for US citizenship. The Trump administration proposes to cap the number of refugees at 30,000 in 2019.

History of U.S. Immigration

In 1924, Congress established national-origin quotas with the Immigration Act of 1924. It awarded immigration visas to just 2 percent of the total number of people of each nationality in the United States as of the 1890 national census. It excluded all immigrants from Asia. People were anxious because of World War I and heartily supported limits on immigration. By 1970, immigration had fallen to a low of 4.7 percent of the population. That was down from a high of 14.7 percent in 1910.

In 1965, President Lyndon Johnson pushed Congress to change immigration policy with the Immigration and Naturalization Act. It eliminated quotas based on nationality. Instead, it favored those with needed skills or who were joining families in the United States. That increased immigration from Asia and Latin America.

In 2014, America welcomed 1.3 million new immigrants. That's up from 1.2 million in 2013. India sent 147,500. China, which sent 131,800 people, and Mexico, at 130,000, were almost tied. So were Canada at 41,200 immigrants and the Philippines at 40,500 individuals.

Today's percentage of immigrants is similar to the late 19th century when almost 15 percent of US residents were immigrants. Most were from Italy, Germany, or Canada. They were tailors, stonemasons, and shopkeepers with skills needed by the United States.

Those who remained in America for at least 15 years were just as likely to own businesses as the native-born. Their children were just as likely to be accountants, engineers, or lawyers.

How Immigration Affects You

Immigrants have driven two-thirds of US economic growth since 2011. They founded 30 percent US firms, including more than 50 percent of startups valued at over $1 billion.

Although they've helped the economy overall, the benefit is largely in certain industries. Immigrants with advanced degrees gravitate toward scientific and technical jobs that don't require high communication.

Newly arrived immigrants have one thing in common that reduces their ability to compete with native-born workers. They generally don't speak English as well. That means they are less likely to take jobs that require strong communication skills. For example, natives in management and media don't face a lot of competition from newly arrived immigrants.

Immigration has a negative effect on workers without a college degree. That's especially true in agriculture and construction. In 2014, immigrants held 43 percent of agricultural jobs. Twenty percent were documented, according to the Pew Research Center. In building and grounds maintenance, 35 percent of the jobs were taken by immigrants. Nineteen percent were documented. In construction, 27 percent of the jobs went to immigrants, and 12 percent were documented.

In those industries, immigration lowers wages and drives out native-born workers in those areas. That pushes native-born workers into jobs like sales and personal services that require superior communication skills. What hurts some workers helps consumers. Immigrants lower the price of goods and services for everyone. That's because they provide low-cost labor that allows companies to reduce the prices of consumer goods.

Immigrants in the workforce pay taxes into Social Security and Medicare. It improves the age dependency ratio. That's the number of working people who support the nation's senior population. The ratio is worsening because the US born population is aging. There aren't as many in the working age population to support them. As more immigrants enter the workforce, the age dependency ratio improves.

Contrary to other claims, immigrants are not more likely to commit crimes than the native-born population.

Future of Immigration

Immigration dropped during the Great Recession and has not returned to pre-recession levels. Instead, immigration from Latin America may continue to weaken. Researchers from the University of California, San Diego, found there are two reasons. First, the economies of Latin American countries continued to improve. As a result, there isn't as much of an income gap between those countries and the United States.

Second, the baby boom continued through the 1970s. There weren't enough jobs to employ all those young workers entering the labor force in the 1990s. But the economies have had enough time to absorb these workers in the last 20 years. As a result, there isn't the same demographic push sending immigrants to the United States.

> *"How to achieve such change—*
> *involving everything from*
> *demographic policies and*
> *transformation of planet-wide*
> *energy, industrial, and agricultural*
> *systems, to North-South and*
> *interfaith relationships and military*
> *postures—is a gigantic challenge*
> *to everyone."*

Overpopulation and Overconsumption Are at the Center of the Environmental Crisis

Paul Ehrlich and Anne H. Ehrlich

In the following viewpoint, written more than a decade ago, well before reports issued that more Americans died than were born in the first year of the Trump administration, Paul Ehrlich and Anne H. Ehrlich warn of dire global consequences due to a combination of overpopulation and a lack of resources. Their pleas revolved around overconsumption, particularly in the United States, as well as environmental concerns, such as the need to find alternatives to damaging fossil fuels. Paul Ehrlich is professor of population studies and professor of biological sciences at Stanford University's Center for Conservation Biology. Anne H. Ehrlich is policy director at the Center for Conservation Biology at Stanford University.

"Too Many People, Too Much Consumption," by Paul Ehrlich and Anne H. Ehrlich, Yale Environment 360, August 4, 2008. Reprinted by permission.

As you read, consider the following questions:

1. Are the views offered by the authors still relevant more than a decade later?
2. How is the subject matter featured in this viewpoint pertinent specifically to Americans?
3. What specific threats to mankind due to overpopulation do the authors cite?

Over some 60 million years, Homo sapiens has evolved into the dominant animal on the planet, acquiring binocular vision, upright posture, large brains, and—most importantly—language with syntax and that complex store of non-genetic information we call culture. However, in the last several centuries we've increasingly been using our relatively newly acquired power, especially our culturally evolved technologies, to deplete the natural capital of Earth—in particular its deep, rich agricultural soils, its groundwater stored during ice ages, and its biodiversity—as if there were no tomorrow.

The point, all too often ignored, is that this trend is being driven in large part by a combination of population growth and increasing per capita consumption, and it cannot be long continued without risking a collapse of our now-global civilization. Too many people—and especially too many politicians and business executives—are under the delusion that such a disastrous end to the modern human enterprise can be avoided by technological fixes that will allow the population and the economy to grow forever. But if we fail to bring population growth and over-consumption under control—the number of people on Earth is expected to grow from 6.5 billion today to 9 billion by the second half of the 21st century—then we will inhabit a planet where life becomes increasingly untenable because of two looming crises: global heating, and the degradation of the natural systems on which we all depend.

Our species' negative impact on our own life-support systems can be approximated by the equation I=PAT. In that equation, the size of the population (P) is multiplied by the average affluence or consumption per individual (A), and that in turn is multiplied by some measure of the technology (T) that services and drives the consumption. Thus commuting in automobiles powered by subsidized fossil fuels on proliferating freeways creates a much greater T factor than commuting on bikes using simple paths or working at home on a computer network. The product of P, A, and T is Impact (I), a rough estimate of how much humanity is degrading the ecosystem services it depends upon.

The equation is not rocket science. Two billion people, all else being equal, put more greenhouse gases into the atmosphere than one billion people. Two billion rich people disrupt the climate more than two billion poor people. Three hundred million Americans consume more petroleum than 1.3 billion Chinese. And driving an SUV is using a far more environmentally malign transportation technology than riding mass transit.

The technological dimensions of our predicament—such as the need for alternatives to fossil fuel energy—are frequently discussed if too little acted upon. Judging from media reports and the statements of politicians, environmental problems, to the degree they are recognized, can be solved by minor changes in technologies and recycling (T). Switching to ultra-light, fuel-efficient cars will obviously give some short-term advantage, but as population and consumption grow, they will pour still more carbon dioxide (and vaporized rubber) into the atmosphere and require more natural areas to be buried under concrete. More recycling will help, but many of our society's potentially most dangerous effluents (such as hormone-mimicking chemicals) cannot practically be recycled. There is no technological change we can make that will permit growth in either human numbers or material affluence to continue to expand. In the face of this, the neglect of the intertwined issues of population and consumption is stunning.

Many past human societies have collapsed under the weight of overpopulation and environmental neglect, but today the civilization in peril is global. The population factor in what appears to be a looming catastrophe is even greater than most people suppose. Each person added today to the population on average causes more damage to humanity's critical life-support systems than did the previous addition—everything else being equal. The reason is simple: Homo sapiens became the dominant animal by being smart. Farmers didn't settle first on poor soils where water was scarce, but rather in rich river valleys. That's where most cities developed, where rich soils are now being paved over for roads and suburbs, and where water supplies are being polluted or overexploited.

As a result, to support additional people it is necessary to move to ever poorer lands, drill wells deeper, or tap increasingly remote sources to obtain water—and then spend more energy to transport that water ever greater distances to farm fields, homes, and factories. Our distant ancestors could pick up nearly pure copper on Earth's surface when they started to use metals; now people must use vast amounts of energy to mine and smelt gigantic amounts of copper ore of ever poorer quality, some in concentrations of less than one percent. The same can be said for other important metals. And petroleum can no longer be found easily on or near the surface, but must be gleaned from wells drilled a mile or more deep, often in inaccessible localities, such as under continental shelves beneath the sea. All of the paving, drilling, fertilizer manufacturing, pumping, smelting, and transporting needed to provide for the consumption of burgeoning numbers of people produces greenhouse gases and thus tightens the connection between population and climate disruption.

So why is the topic of overpopulation so generally ignored? There are some obvious reasons. Attempts by governments to limit their nation's population growth are anathema to those on the right who believe the only role for governments in the bedroom is to force women to take unwanted babies to term. Those on the left fear, with some legitimacy, that population control could turn racist or discriminatory in other ways—for example, attempting to reduce the numbers of minorities or the poor. Many fear the specter of more of "them" compared to "us," and all of us fear loss of liberty and economic decline (since population growth is often claimed necessary for economic health). And there are religious leaders who still try to promote over-reproduction by their flocks, though in much of the world their efforts are largely futile (Catholic countries in Europe tend to be low-birthrate leaders, for example).

But much of the responsibility must go to ignorance, which leads mainstream media, even newspapers like The New York Times, to maintain a pro-natalist stance. For example, the Times had an article on June 29 about a "baby bust" in industrialized countries in which the United States (still growing) was noted as a "sparkling exception." Beyond the media, great foundations have turned their "population programs" away from encouraging low fertility rates and toward topics like "changing sexual mores"— avoiding discussion of the contribution demographics is making to a possible collapse of civilization.

Silence on the overconsumption (Affluence) factor in the I=PAT equation is more readily explained. Consumption is still viewed as an unalloyed good by many economists, along with business leaders and politicians, who tend to see jacking up consumption as a cure-all for economic ills. Too much unemployment? Encourage people to buy an SUV or a new refrigerator. Perpetual growth is the creed of the cancer cell, but third-rate economists can't think of anything else. Some leading economists are starting to tackle the issue of overconsumption, but the problem and its cures are tough to analyze. Scientists have yet to develop consumption condoms or morning-after-shopping-spree pills.

And, of course, there are the vexing problems of consumption of people in poor countries. On one hand, a billion or more people have problems of underconsumption. Unless their basic needs are met, they are unlikely to be able to make important contributions to attaining sustainability. On the other hand, there is also the issue of the "new consumers" in developing economies such as China and India, where the wealth of a sizable minority is permitting them to acquire the consumption habits (e.g., eating a lot of meat and driving automobiles) of the rich nations. Consumption regulation is a lot more complex than population regulation, and it is much more difficult to find humane and equitable solutions to the problem.

The dominant animal is wasting its brilliance and its wonderful achievements; civilization's fate is being determined by decision makers who determinedly look the other way in favor of immediate comfort and profit. Thousands of scientists recently participated in a Millennium Ecosystem Assessment that outlined our current environmental dilemma, but the report's dire message made very little impact. Absent attention to that message, the fates of Easter Island, the Classic Maya civilization, and Nineveh—all of which collapsed following environmental degradation—await us all.

We believe it is possible to avoid that global denouement. Such mobilization means developing some consensus on goals—perhaps through a global dialogue in which people discuss the human predicament and decide whether they would like to see a maximum number of people living at a minimum standard of living, or perhaps a much lower population size that gives individuals a broad choice of lifestyles. We have suggested a forum for such a dialogue, modeled partly on the Intergovernmental Panel on Climate Change, but with more "bottom up" participation. It is clear that only widespread changes in norms can give humanity a chance of attaining a sustainable and reasonably conflict-free society.

How to achieve such change—involving everything from demographic policies and transformation of planet-wide energy, industrial, and agricultural systems, to North-South and interfaith relationships and military postures—is a gigantic challenge to everyone. Politicians, industrialists, ecologists, social scientists, everyday citizens, and the media must join this debate. Whether it is possible remains to be seen; societies have managed to make major transitions in the recent past, as the civil rights revolution in the United States and the collapse of communism in the Soviet Union clearly demonstrate.

We'll continue to hope and work for a cultural transformation in how we treat each other and the natural systems we depend upon. We can create a peaceful and sustainable global civilization, but it will require realistic thinking about the problems we face and a new mobilization of political will.

> "A free society with social rules enables people to exercise their talents for their own sakes. This inevitably benefits others by bringing forth prodigious productive efforts which cause growth. And each generation creates a little bit more than it uses. Hence each new generation is richer than the previous generation."

Population Growth Benefits the Environment

Julian Simon

In the following viewpoint, an interview in Religion & Liberty, *a quarterly journal of religion, economics, and culture, Julian Simon offers a rebuttal to those who believe population growth has a negative effect on the environment. The author cites how those in the most densely populated areas of the world are those that are thriving. He sees population control as morally wrong. He makes it apparent in the interview that his views are based on his strong religious beliefs, but he also provides statistics to back his opinions. Julian Simon is an author at the Acton Institute.*

"Population Growth Benefits the Environment," by Julian Simon, Acton Institute, July 20, 2010.

As you read, consider the following questions:

1. What is the strongest point made in the viewpoint connecting population growth and a positive impact on the environment?
2. Does the author espouse unlimited global population growth?
3. How strongly do Simon's religious beliefs factor into the opinions he offers?

Religion & Liberty: You have written extensively on the subject of population growth. Could you explain the thesis of your argument that population growth and density are beneficial for countries in the long run.

Simon: Population growth does not have a statistically negative effect upon economic growth. We know that from 30 years of careful quantitative scientific studies—just the opposite of what the public believes. Because human knowledge allows us to produce more finished products out of fewer raw materials, natural resources are becoming more available. The air and water in rich countries are becoming cleaner. Most importantly, human beings are living much longer than ever before.

R&L: Yet we hear the fear that if there are too many people who consume the resources of a given society, life there will become untenable.

Simon: You say this while we are here in Cannes, a densely populated city, measured by the number of persons per square mile. But if we were to look inside those hotel rooms to see how much space those people have, we would see that they are living with luxurious amounts of space. People have more and better living space than ever before. If we array the countries of the world according to population density, and then look at the rate of economic growth, we see that it is the more densely-populated countries—such as Hong Kong, Singapore, Holland, Japan—that are growing faster, and that the less-densely populated countries— such as those in Africa—are growing at slower rates.

The view that I have expressed to you thus far is precisely the view held by experts on these topics. Every agricultural economist knows that people have been eating better since World War II, the period for which we have data. Every resource economist knows that natural resources have become cheaper rather than more expensive. Every demographer knows that life expectancy in the wealthy countries has gone up from under 30 years at birth 200 years ago to over 75 years at birth today. And life expectancy has risen in the poor countries from perhaps 35 years at birth only 50 years ago to 60-65-70 years at birth today. Those are the facts which are known by the economists and demographers who study these subjects.

R&L: If that is the case, then how do you explain the popular view on that subject?

Simon: For the past 25 years, whenever I would give people the facts about population and resources, they would say, "Well then, why do we hear so much bad news?" And for 25 years I have been struggling to work out the answers. The question is extraordinarily complex. The influences range from a genetic propensity deep in human nature to prophesy bad news to a lot of everyday factors such as the media's tendency to seek out and report bad news.

R&L: Share some thoughts on your debate with Paul Ehrlich, who made the "population bomb" thesis popular.

Simon: I remember my reaction in 1970 when seeing Ehrlich for a full hour on Johnny Carson's television show. Carson said something like, "Paul, explain the population problem to me." And Ehrlich answered, "Johnny, it's really very simple." At that time I was not sure exactly what the answer to the problem was, but the one thing I was absolutely certain of was that it is not simple. As a result of that debate I began to see that part of the problem is our "common-sensical" approach to problems which inevitably over-simplifies a complex problem like this.

Malthusian common sense is a very attractive idea. But the heart of the growth of civilizations and economies is the non-Malthusian adjustment process that is inevitably complex, and indeed counter-intuitive. The common-sensical Malthusian view sees only the short term rather than the long term. But in the long term these adjustment processes tend to produce opposite results to what the short term results happen to be. Here we should note that science is only interesting when it produces results which are the opposite of common sense. Otherwise you wouldn't need scientists at all.

R&L: It is rather similar to the difficulty of making classical liberal ideas popular as compared to statist or socialist ideas. The latter seem more easily condensed to a bumper sticker.

Simon: Absolutely. That is one of the reasons for their great success. The underlying ideas of socialism are marvelously attractive-for example, the idea of economies of scale that bewitched Marx: Remove the waste of having six competing steel mills and the advertising and marketing which accompany them. Combine them sounds good. But the opposite results occur. Yet this simple-minded idea bewitches people such as Andre Sakarov, Albert Einstein, Bertrand Russell and others who are marvelously clear and penetrating thinkers in other spheres of life. But in this sphere-if you will permit me-they are just plain stupid.

R&L: What indications of coercion in family planning do you find in the official Cairo Conference documents?

Simon: The UNFPA people have learned over the years to be extremely careful to frequently mouth platitudes such as "everything is voluntary." At the same time, they espouse goals in population growth. The idea of goals and the idea of voluntarism are fundamentally contradictory. If you are attempting to require some level of population growth, whether it be zero population growth or two percent population growth, inevitably you will have to do something to people to get them to that stage, unless they will do it themselves. If they will do it themselves, then you do not need a population conference or UNFPA. So inherent in the idea of stabilization of population, or any positive growth rate, is the idea of coercion.

R&L: In China there have been coercive family planning policies in place for some time, including forced abortions. What kind of arguments do you give against state efforts to coerce couples into having families of a certain size?

Simon: The first reason I oppose these coercive policies is because they are morally wrong. They deny individual liberty in one of the most important choices a couple may make—the number of children they will have. So I would be against this coercion even if there were an economic rationale for it. The most tragic aspect of the matter is that there is no economic warrant for forcing people to have fewer children.

It may be true that under socialism or communism, as in China, it takes longer for additional people to receive benefits, and the benefits of additional people are less than those in a capitalist system. It would be better if China would shift to a system where people were free in all ways, including economically free. Additional children then would more quickly benefit others then now. Still, there is no economic warrant to limit population growth even in contemporary China.

R&L: What are the main causes of poverty in developing nations if population growth is not a major factor?

Simon: By 1994 we have solid statistical evidence about the determinants of economic development. What could only be said on economic faith 30 years ago, we can now document scientifically. We now know statistically that what David Hume wrote on the subject in the 1700s was exactly right. When identifying why Holland was the richest country in Europe, Hume said that "Liberty, necessity, and a multitude of people" were the causes.

A free society with social rules enables people to exercise their talents for their own sakes. This inevitably benefits others by bringing forth prodigious productive efforts which cause growth. And each generation creates a little bit more than it uses. Hence each new generation is richer than the previous generation.

This process is made more rapid by a free society. We frequently hear in the press how people in rich countries, such as the United States, constitute only five percent of the population and use up 40 percent of the resources. That may be true, but people in rich countries make available even more than 40 percent of the resources.

R&L: Give us an overview of your thoughts on immigration policy.

Simon: Immigrants are human beings above all, and more human beings are beneficial because of their minds and the goods their minds produce. Immigrants also have additional beneficial properties because they usually migrate when they are young and strong. Therefore, in a welfare society such as the United States which taxes some and gives others benefits, immigrants are large net contributors to the public coffers. Thus we benefit greatly from immigrants.

R&L: Tell us how important the Sabbath is to you. Does it have a connection to the contents of this interview?

Simon: Though in no sense am I a conventional orthodox Jew, I do observe the Sabbath by refraining from all work, and by celebrating the Sabbath in life. And almost every Sabbath when weather permits—nearly half the Saturdays in the year in Washington—I sit outside in the garden behind my house, amidst both the glories of nature, and the beautiful homes of others. I admire and am thrilled by how both the natural and the man-made come together to make our dwelling place a more beautiful spot than wild nature alone.

> "The annual population increase of
> over 80 million equates to a city
> for 1.5 million people having to be
> built, somewhere, every week—with,
> inevitably, ever more greenhouse
> gas emissions and the continuing
> destruction of forests and wetlands,
> with their multiple habitats
> for the web of life on which all
> species depend."

There Are Not Enough Resources to Support the World's Population

John Guillebaud

In the following viewpoint, John Guillebaud argues that the world population has soared to the point (above seven billion) that there is a lack of resources to care for it. He warns that Earth does not boast infinite resources and cites Worldwide Fund for Nature estimates that by the year 2050, humankind will require 100 percent more of the planet's total biocapacity, such as forestry, fisheries, and croplands, to feed and house all the people. He even laments jokingly that earthlings might need to find another planet to plunder in the distant future. The author notes that the data in this viewpoint was accurate at the time it was written, but it is important to seek the latest numbers. John Guillebaud is Emeritus Professor of Family Planning and Reproductive Health at University College London.

"There Are Not Enough Resources to Support the World's Population," by John Guillebaud, ABC.net, June 10, 2014. Reprinted by permission.

As you read, consider the following questions:

1. How does this viewpoint use data to explore the problem and solutions?
2. What suggestions does the author give to individuals in their daily lives that could help alleviate the problems caused by a growing world population?
3. What are some of the sustainable resources the author reports to be lacking?

M any years ago, as a second year medical student, I attended a lecture on human population by my tutor at Cambridge, Colin Bertram. He argued as a biologist that relentless population increase by any species is always ultimately unsustainable; numbers increase to the limits of the carrying capacity of their environment and when they overshoot this, their numbers always collapse. If we allow unremitting population growth to continue we humans cannot escape the same fate; however cleverly we might adapt to all the different environments on earth, we only have one finite planet to live on and 70 per cent of it is salt water, and half of the remainder is desert, mountain, icecap or fast-disappearing forest.

Dr Bertram's lecture startled me and established the direction of my medical career. I felt some guilt that doctors had inadvertently caused the population problem through vastly better death control while birth rates remained high. I decided that, as an about-to-be doctor, I should try to restore balance, and what more appropriate medical specialty could there be than family planning? So I arranged higher training in gynaecology (specialising in hormonal and intrauterine contraception) and also in surgery (hence my career total of 5000 vasectomies and ongoing research into a new male pill).

None of us in those days was worried specifically about climate change. As we've just been reminded by the Intergovernmental Panel on Climate Change, that environmental problem is terrifying enough, especially given the risk of runaway positive feedbacks, caused, for example, by methane release from permafrost. Even so, that is far from being the only life-threatening global problem. The UK government's chief scientist and the last president of the Royal Society have highlighted the imminence of a "perfect storm": water, food and fossil fuel scarcity. Reliable reports on the planet's health such as The United Nations' *Global Environment Outlook* have found water, land, plants, animals and fish stocks are all 'in inexorable decline'. Already by 2002 it was calculated that 97 per cent of all vertebrate flesh on land was human flesh plus that of our food animals (cows, pigs, sheep etc), leaving just three per cent for all wild vertebrate species on land. Not to mention the obliteration of wild life in the oceans through acidification, pollution and massive over-fishing.

Regarding human numbers there is some good news: the total fertility rate or average family size of the world has halved since 1950, when it was over five, to about 2.5 (where 2.1 would be replacement level). The bad news is that despite this, the 58 highest fertility countries are projected to triple their numbers by 2100. In a majority of all countries there is also persistent population momentum created by 'bulges' of young people born in high fertility years.

Therefore, the UN warns bluntly that world population, now well over seven billion "has reached a stage where the amount of resources needed to sustain it exceeds what is available." The annual population increase of over 80 million equates to a city for 1.5 million people having to be built, somewhere, every week— with, inevitably, ever more greenhouse gas emissions and the continuing destruction of forests and wetlands, with their multiple habitats for the web of life on which all species depend.

This is not exactly a bundle of laughs, yet it is solidly evidence-based, as any impartial scientific observer will attest. Those who are not so impartial routinely prefer to "shoot the messenger" or behave like an ostrich.

The Worldwide Fund for Nature calculates that by 2050, humankind will need 100 per cent more of the planet's total biocapacity (forestry, fisheries, croplands) than there is. What are the prospects of finding another planet for humans to plunder by 2050? On a finite planet sustainability is not an option, it's just a matter of how it is achieved. Will the imbalance be corrected by literally billions of deaths or by fewer births? How strange, given the evidence, that population growth and contraception remain largely taboo.

Those who consume way beyond their share, the rich over-consumers in every country, must certainly massively reduce their environmental footprints, but the "number of feet" is also relevant. Often statements like this are assumed to refer to the poor, but our organisation, Population Matters, stresses that affluent parents must also seriously consider having one less child than they may have planned. The guideline is just two for replacement.

All this is hardly rocket science: indeed you could hardly have a better example of Ockham's razor. Surely, continuing business as usual involves far more unrealistically optimistic assumptions than the precautionary approach. The precautionary approach requires proper resourcing of voluntary family planning services, which still receive a derisory less than one per cent of world aid for reproductive health, and the removal through education and the media of the many barriers that continue to stop millions of women from having the choice to access methods of contraception. This is not an alternative to the other crucial precautionary measure: reducing the size of humanity's mean environmental footprint. Both are vital; they are two sides of the same coin.

When the camel collapses with a broken back, the last straw did not really do it. It was the fault of all the straws. To achieve environmental sustainability, everyone must be involved.

When a field of common land is right at the point of being over-grazed, Garret Hardin called it "the tragedy of the commons." This is because each herdsman continues to find it advantageous, personally and for his family, to put yet one more cow on the land, and another and another—even if the later new arrivals are thinner and less productive than before—right up to the point that the grazing limit is finally exceeded and all the cows die and all the families suffer. Fishermen behave similarly when there is a nearly over-exploited fishery. Given any resource that is held in common, the private gain of the individual is thus at the shared cost of the whole group, progressively and ultimately catastrophically.

Hardin said the way to avoid these tragedies was "mutual coercion, mutually agreed upon," meaning everyone agreeing to be regulated by peer-pressure, along with agreed fiscal incentives and disincentives. So in the fishery example, each fisherman takes an agreed smaller quota, which is sustainable. However, not every relevant thing that happens in the environmental commons can be so regulated. The multiple decisions made by each individual about cycling or walking rather than going by car, switching off air conditioners or choosing to have a small family are difficult to influence. When push comes to shove—especially when we see so much continuing gluttony in energy use by large corporations—all of us can feel wonder what the point of helping the environment is when it seems like nobody else does.

Which brings me to my own project, the Eco Time Capsule. Generally, time capsules record a particular time and place for posterity, and are buried without any future date for unearthing in mind. The time capsules we buried in 1994 were different. The concept came to me through that well-known saying: "We have not inherited the earth from our grandparents, we have borrowed it from our grandchildren." I reflected on how angry our grandchildren are likely to be if we continue to wreck their loan to us. With 25 years as the usually accepted average duration of a generation, our grandchildren would be people living 50 years ahead. So this project was addressed to the people of 2044.

The time capsules contained environmentally-relevant items and were buried with letters of apology at significant sites around the world: in the Kew Gardens in London and Ness Gardens near Liverpool, in Mexico, Pietermaritzburg in South Africa, the Seychelles and at Mount Annan near Sydney.

Children were—and still are—central to this project, since they are the prime stakeholders for a decent, sustainable future. In 1994 more than 1,000 entered two competitions, one for the best brief letter or poem addressed to the finder in 2044; the other for the most striking and original ideas for appropriate artefacts to go in the capsules. My own choices for sustainability symbols were a bicycle pump and a packet of contraceptive pills.

We felt it was essential to apologise. However, more important and empowering was the pledge to do everything possible to save the planet by individual and united action. The goal is that the finders of the capsules in the year 2044 will wonder why we apologised.

> "Today, college remains the greatest
> driver of socioeconomic mobility in
> America, but if we don't do more
> to keep it within reach for middle-
> class families and those striving to
> get into the middle class, it could
> have the opposite effect—serving as
> a barrier, instead of as a ticket to the
> American Dream."

Student Loan Debt Has Become a Barrier to a Quality Education

US Department of Education

In the following viewpoint, written during the Obama adminstration, the US Department of Education argues that young people are being saddled with student debt before career opportunities even begin. Universities try to lure prospective students with attractive expansion and modernization, thereby sending tuition costs skyrocketing, but many students never see a return on their investment, as crippling debts of student loans fail to offset earned wages. Some on the left of the political spectrum call for a policy of free tuition for all students, which would force universities to provide access to millions of youth that simply cannot afford a quality education. The US Department of Education is a cabinet-level department of the US government concerned with assistance to education.

"College Affordability and Completion: Ensuring a Pathway to Opportunity," US Department of Education.

As you read, consider the following questions:

1. How distressing is the fear that many Americans do not have equal access to higher education according to the viewpoint?
2. Do you believe that equal college opportunities is more of a moral issue or one that harms the American economy?
3. What statistics does the Department of Education give to sound the alarm about crippling student debt?

Creating a clear path to the middle class and ensuring our nation's economic prosperity means opening the doors of higher education to more Americans. Today, three-quarters of the fastest-growing occupations require education and training beyond a high school diploma. Yet nearly half the students who begin college in this country don't finish within six years. And tuition continues to rise, putting college out of reach for the very families that need it most to join the middle class. A generation ago, America led the world in college attainment of young adults; now, we rank 13th. The Obama administration is committed to restoring our world leadership in college completion and ensuring that every student has access to an affordable and high-quality postsecondary education.

College Is More Important—But More Expensive—Than Ever Before

A Postsecondary Credential Has Never Been More Important
In today's economy, higher education is no longer a luxury for the privileged few, but a necessity for individual economic opportunity and America's competitiveness in the global economy. At a time when jobs can go anywhere in the world, skills and education will determine success for individuals and for nations. As a result, a college education remains the best investment a student can make in his or her future.

- College graduates with a bachelor's degree typically earn 66 percent more than those with only a high school diploma; and are also far less likely to face unemployment.
- Over the course of a lifetime, the average worker with a bachelor's degree will earn approximately $1 million more than a worker without a postsecondary education.
- By 2020, an estimated two-thirds of job openings will require postsecondary education or training.

Students—including many older students juggling work and family responsibilities—recognize that higher education is a key to opportunity, and that has fueled a substantial increase in college enrollment rates in recent years. But unfortunately, for millions of other students, our higher education system isn't delivering what they need, or deserve. In part because of the rising costs of college, too many students are unable to enroll or complete high-quality degrees.

College Has Never Been More Expensive

- Even as a college degree or other postsecondary credential or certificate has never been more important, it has also never been more expensive. Over the past three decades, tuition at public four-year colleges has more than doubled, even after adjusting for inflation.
- Between 1992 and 2012, the average amount owed by a typical student loan borrower who graduated with a bachelor's degree more than doubled to a total of nearly $27,000.
- Even after historic investments by the Obama Administration, the maximum Pell Grant covers only about 30 percent of the cost of a four-year public college education—the lowest proportion in history and less than half of what it covered in 1980. Despite that fact, Congressional Republicans have proposed to cut the real purchasing power of Pell Grants even further.

Too many recent college graduates feel the weight of their student loan payments holding them back from fulfilling their full potential. And far too many prospective college students feel as though they are simply priced out of the education they need to set themselves up for future success. There is a significant opportunity gap as well. While half of Americans from high-income families hold a bachelor's degree by age 25, just 1 in 10 people from low-income families attain that level of education. Moreover, regardless of income status, high-school graduates who enroll in college too often fail to finish: barely half will complete their degree in a reasonable time at four-year institutions; and at two-year schools it's only about a third.

Today, college remains the greatest driver of socioeconomic mobility in America, but if we don't do more to keep it within reach for middle-class families and those striving to get into the middle class, it could have the opposite effect—serving as a barrier, instead of as a ticket to the American Dream. Every hard-working student deserves a real opportunity to earn an affordable, high-quality degree or credential that offers a clear path to civic engagement, economic security, and success.

Historic Investments in College Affordability

Since taking office in 2009, the Obama Administration has taken strong action to counteract the rising cost of higher education, expanding Pell Grants and making student debt more manageable by expanding loan repayment options that cap payments based on income. Putting in place the largest investment in higher education funding since the GI bill, the Administration has increased total annual aid to students by over $50 billion from 2008 to 2016, and selected annual tax benefits by over $12 billion, which has helped our nation ensure more students are graduating college than ever before.

- In 2010, the Obama Administration and Congress made a landmark investment in Pell Grants, ending student loan subsidies for private banks and shifting over $60 billion in savings back to students and taxpayers.

- This Administration has raised the maximum Pell Grant award by more than $1,000 since 2008, and for the first time, tied it to inflation. Under the President's leadership, the number of Pell Grant recipients has expanded by one-third over that same time, providing college access to millions of additional low-income and middle-class students across the country.

- The Administration also established and extended the American Opportunity Tax Credit to assist families with the costs of college, providing up to $10,000 for four years of college tuition, which has helped 10 million students and families afford college.

- Last year, the President unveiled his America's College Promise proposal to make two years of community college free for responsible students to earn critical workforce skills and the first half of a bachelor's degree at no cost.

The Administration also has worked to help Americans manage their student loan debt. In addition to fighting to reduce student loan interest rates, saving students up to $1,000, the Administration has improved and expanded income-driven loan repayment options, ensuring that all Direct Loan borrowers can cap their payments at ten percent of their discretionary income and that loan payments are manageable. As late as mid-2012, fewer than a million borrowers were in income-driven repayment plans. The Administration's expansion effort has nearly quadrupled participation, and delinquencies and defaults are down.

Doing More to Focus on Student Outcomes

Cost and Debt Are Only Part of the Story—We
Need Increased Focus on Student Success

Addressing growing college costs and debt is absolutely critical. Many more students need access to vastly more affordable and quality higher education opportunities—including tuition-free degree options. For too long, though, America's higher education system has focused almost exclusively on inputs—enrolling students in college—and too little on outcomes—graduating from college with high-quality degrees. We must reset the incentives that underpin the system so the focus is on the outcome that matters: completing a quality degree at a reasonable cost. Otherwise, we will merely be finding better ways of paying for an unsustainable status quo.

The Most Expensive Education Is One That Doesn't Lead to a Degree

While graduating with high levels of debt is holding too many borrowers back from reaching their full potential, the even more damaging outcome is for students who take on debt but never complete their degree. In fact, students' ability to repay their loans depends more strongly on whether they graduate than on how much total debt they take on.

- Students who take out college loans but don't graduate are three times more likely to default than borrowers who complete.
- The median debt of borrowers who default is under $8,900, which is barely half of the median debt load for all students.
- States with the highest default rates for their four-year colleges tend to be near the bottom on completion rates too; and states with the lowest default rates tend to rank higher in four-year completion rates.
- More than 40 percent of first-time, full-time students who enroll in a bachelor's degree program don't graduate within 6 years.
- Low-income students, first-generation college students, and minority students, in particular, are being underserved by the current system. Just 9 percent of students from the lowest income quartile graduate with a bachelor's degree by age 24, compared to 77 percent for the top income quartile.

- Students from low-income families are also less likely to enroll in and complete college than their peers, even when academic ability is taken into consideration.

The Obama Administration Is Shifting the Conversation Toward Outcomes

Over the past seven years, the Administration has pursued executive actions and put forward policy proposals to address structural flaws in the higher education system and create incentives for all actors to focus on student outcomes:

- Through its landmark Gainful Employment regulations, the Obama Administration is stopping the flow of federal dollars to low-performing career college programs that leave students buried in debt with few opportunities to repay it.
- And in 2015, the Department announced executive actions and legislative proposals to strengthen accreditation, the stamp of approval that colleges need before accessing federal financial aid. Together, these actions build on the work that the Administration has done to ensure that higher education institutions are effectively serving students and families while staying accountable to taxpayer dollars.
- The Administration also has proposed encouraging students to complete their studies on time by strengthening academic progress requirements in federal student aid programs.
- The Administration has greatly increased transparency for students and families so that they can make informed decisions through tools like the College Scorecard and the Financial Aid Shopping Sheet and choose a school that is affordable, best-suited to meet their needs, and consistent with their educational and career goals. The College Scorecard, in particular, represents the next generation of college transparency: providing students and families with more data than ever before to help them compare college

costs and outcomes as they search for the college that is right for them.

Much Work Remains for All Involved

Despite the Administration's historic actions and the leadership of innovative institutions, much work remains to meet our goal of once again having the highest proportion of college graduates in the world. The Administration will continue to act within its power to improve college access, affordability, and completion, but we also need Congress, states, colleges and universities, and accreditors to join in that effort.

We must encourage states to reverse a quarter-century-long trend of disinvestment in higher education, promote reforms to support student success, and embrace their role in overseeing institutions. Thirty states already fund institutions to some extent based on performance indicators and several others are transitioning to such systems. We need to build on that momentum and progress.

States also must align their secondary and postsecondary systems, reform remedial education, and ensure seamless transitions into college and among institutions by making it easy to transfer credits. And they must take seriously their historical role in consumer protection through a robust authorization and oversight process, as well as active monitoring of compliance of institutions doing business in their state.

We must encourage accreditors to focus on student outcomes, raise the bar for quality, and promote transparency. Accreditors must offer new levels of transparency and quality assurance based on outcomes—not just inputs. We must encourage institutions to improve their performance by recognizing and rewarding colleges with strong student outcomes, especially with the neediest students, and incentivizing underperforming colleges to improve. All institutions and systems must do more to control costs and innovate to make degrees more affordable, and focus on their success rate with students who have traditionally been least likely to complete their programs and degrees. And for those that are ultimately more concerned about their bottom lines than about their students, we should stop the flow of taxpayer dollars.

In addition to supporting these needed changes, Congress must do more to protect students from unscrupulous career colleges that deceive students into taking on debt they will never be able to repay and then stick taxpayers with the bill. We must strengthen, not weaken, accountability in higher education. For too long, Congress has sat on the sideline—or worse, actively fought—the Administration's efforts to protect students and taxpayers from these predatory and deceptive practices. While urging Congress to act, the Department has taken additional steps in the past year to offer greater safeguards for students and better support for borrowers.

Support for Higher Education in the Fiscal Year 2017 Budget

The 2017 budget continues on the path of helping to ensure that students can attain a postsecondary credential without taking on more debt than they and their families can afford. It also supports an ongoing shift toward focusing on student outcomes in higher education, and, in particular, completion, so that both students and the nation can thrive in the global economy. As a result, the 2017 budget includes proposals to address college access, affordability, and completion:

- Funding America's College Promise (ACP): A new partnership with states, this effort would provide $61 billion over the next decade to make two years of community college free for responsible students, so they can earn the first half of a bachelor's degree or an associate degree at no cost. ACP also would fund grants to four-year Historically Black Colleges and Universities (HBCUs) and Minority-Serving Institutions (MSIs) to provide new low-income students and minority students, including community college transfer students, with up to two years of college credits at zero or significantly reduced tuition.

- Strengthening and expanding access to Pell Grants. The President plans to:
  - Ensure full funding for the Pell Grant maximum award (estimated at $5,935 in award year 2017-2018) and to continue indexing the grant to inflation indefinitely, to protect and sustain its value for future generations.

  - Encourage on-time and faster completion through the Pell for Accelerated Completion program, by making Pell Grant funds available year-round to students who are taking a full course load and have exhausted their award.

  - Offer an additional $300 On-Track Pell Bonus for students who take at least 15 credit hours per semester, and are on course to complete college on time.

  - Implement the Second Chance Pell program, enabling prisoners eligible for release to receive Pell Grant funds and access postsecondary opportunities that will help them rejoin society, get good jobs, support their families, and strengthen their communities.

- Launching an HBCU and MSI Innovation for Completion Fund: A new $30 million competitive grant program would support innovative, evidence-based, student-centered strategies to increase the number of low-income students and students of color who earn their degrees.
- Creating a College Opportunity and Graduation Bonus program: This initiative aims to reward colleges that successfully enroll and graduate significant numbers of low-income students on time, and encourage better system-wide performance.

- Advancing innovation through the First in the World initiative: A third round of funding, at $100 million, would enable more partnerships to implement and evaluate promising or proven strategies to increase college success for all students, including low-income, minority, and first-generation learners, including up to $30 million for HBCUs and MSIs.
- Creating an American Technical Training Fund: Through this $75 million effort, jointly administered by the Departments of Education and Labor, partnerships will develop or expand tuition-free, innovative, evidence-based short-term or accelerated job training programs in high-demand fields like health care, manufacturing, and information technology.
- Simplifying the FAFSA by eliminating burdensome and unnecessarily complex questions to make it easier for students and families to access federal student aid and afford a postsecondary education.

Periodical and Internet Sources Bibliography

The following articles have been selected to supplement the diverse views presented in this chapter.

Jillian Berman, "America's $1.5 Trillion Student Loan Industry Is a 'Failed Social Experiment,'" Market Watch, October 18, 2018. https://www.marketwatch.com/story/americas-15-trillion-student-debt-is-a-failed-social-experiment-2018-10-16.

David E. Card, "How Immigration Affects U.S. Cities," Ideas. https://ideas.repec.org/p/crm/wpaper/0711.html.

Chelsea Follett, "How Big of a Problem Is Overpopulation?" *Forbes*, July 30, 2018. https://www.forbes.com/sites/quora/2018/07/30/how-big-of-a-problem-is-overpopulation/#220e61df216a.

Yoram Hazony, "How Americans Lost Their National Identity," *Time*. October 23, 2018. http://time.com/5431089/trump-white-nationalism-bible/.

Kenneth Megan and Theresa Cardinal Brown, "America's Demographic Vhallenge: Understanding the Role of Immigration," Bipartisonpolicy.org. August 2017. https://bipartisanpolicy.org/wp-content/uploads/2017/08/BPC-Immigration-Americas-Demographic-Challenge.pdf.

Robert Paarlberg, "Over-Consumption in America: Beyond Corporate Power, " Oxford University Press, May 31, 2015. https://blog.oup.com/2015/05/over-consumption-america-corporate-power/.

Christopher L. Peterson and Cliff A. Robb, "The Student Debt Crisis: Could It Slow the U.S. Economy? Wharton University of Pennsylvania, October 22, 2018. https://knowledge.wharton.upenn.edu/article/student-loan-debt-crisis/.

Lyman Stone, "Why You Shouldn't Obsess About 'Overpopulation,'" Vox, July 11, 2018. https://www.vox.com/the-big-idea/2017/12/12/16766872/overpopulation-exaggerated-concern-climate-change-world-population.

Matthew Sussis, "Five Ways Immigration-Driven Population Growth Impacts Our Environment," Center for Immigration Studies, November 19, 2018. https://cis.org/Sussis/Five-Ways-ImmigrationDriven-Population-Growth-Impacts-Our-Environment.

OPPOSING VIEWPOINTS® SERIES

CHAPTER 4

What Is America's Electoral Future?

Chapter Preface

The election of Barack Obama to the presidency in 2008 was a historical moment. An African American president was something many Americans thought they would never see, given the country's thorny history with race. Suddenly, it seemed, America had finally shed its narrow thinking of the past and its voters were looking toward a new age, a future full of possibility Many hoped the momentum could continue in 2016, with the election of the United States's first woman president, but instead Americans voted for a white male once again.

Still, Americans voted an unprecedented number of women, people of color, and LGBTQ candidates into office during the 2018 midterm elections. The representatives in Congress as well as leaders of local and state governments are beginning to look a lot more like the current makeup of America. There is no reason to think this progress will backslide in the future, as a younger and more diverse generation of Americans cast their votes.

As white Americans age and die off and a new vision of America emerges, views on political issues and the leaders elected to address them will undoubtedly change. The viewpoints in the following chapter examine the tension that many predict will cloud the political landscape as this cultural shift occurs in the next few decades. Authors offer predictions for what we might be able to expect, whether it's a more progressive America, a backlash into more conservative outlooks, or a radical change to our entire system.

> *"The increased growth of new minorities—Hispanics and Asians and persons of two or more races—has begun to make its mark on the nation's electorate by reducing the white portion of total voters."*

America's Diversity Explosion Is Changing the Political Landscape

William H. Frey

In the following viewpoint William H. Frey provides a statistical analysis of how demographic shifts in the United States, particularly the increasing number of racial minorities and decrease in the white electorate, has impacted elections such as those in 2008 and 2012 that landed and kept Barack Obama in office. The author adds, however, that minorities such as Hispanics and Asians are less likely to vote than their white and African American counterparts. William H. Frey is a senior fellow with the Brookings Institution and research professor in population studies at the University of Michigan.

As you read, consider the following questions:

1. Did the author's argument about diversity affecting the political landscape take a hit when Donald Trump won the presidency in 2016?
2. From what two international regions do immigrant groups have an increasing impact on voting in American elections, according to the viewpoint?
3. Does the author indicate that the political shifts he foresees will benefit Democrats or Republicans?

T he sweeping diversity explosion now underway in the US will continue to impact the political landscape as the racial profiles of the electorate and voters continue to change.[1] Testament to this is the election of the nation's first black president, Barack Obama, which can be attributed, in large part, to a growing minority electorate both nationally and in previously Republican-leaning Sun Belt states. This article reviews the nation's new racial demographic shifts with an eye to how it has changed the electorate and outcomes of the past three presidential elections, and suggesting what it may mean for the future.

Rising Racial Diversity Among the US Population and Voters

The increased growth of new minorities—Hispanics and Asians and persons of two or more races—has begun to make its mark on the nation's electorate by reducing the white portion of total voters. As recently as the 1980 presidential election, racial minorities comprised less than 10 percent of voters, compared with fully 26 percent in 2012. Yet the minority share of voters was still lower than its share of the total US population, which was 37 percent.

The reason for this discrepancy between the racial makeup of voters and the population might be termed a "voter representation gap." A large part of this gap for Hispanics and Asians is attributable to two factors. First, compared with whites, more Hispanics in

America are under 18 years of age and are, therefore, too young to vote. Second, even among those Hispanics and Asians who are old enough to vote, a smaller share have become citizens, even if they reside in the United States legally.

As a consequence, the portion of all Hispanics and Asians who are eligible to vote—citizens age 18 and above—constituted only about one-half or less of their total populations. (See Figure A.) This contrasts with blacks and whites, of whom 69 percent and 79 percent of their respective populations were eligible to vote.

[There is a] lag in translating the Hispanic and Asian representation in the total population to the population that is eligible to vote. For example, the Hispanic portion of the total population increased from 14 to 17 percent between the 2004 and 2012 elections. Yet, its portion of eligible voters increased from

Figure A: Share of Population Eligible to Vote, 2012

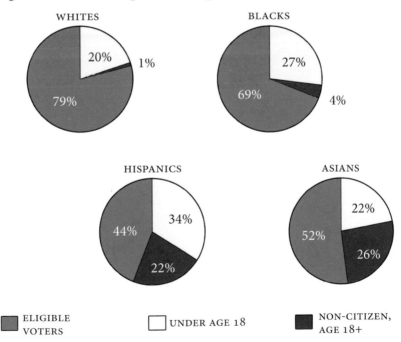

Source: William H. Frey, *Diversity Explosion: How New Racial Demographics Are Remaking America* (Brookings Institution Press, 2015).

just 8 to 11 percent, respectively. In contrast, whites are more highly represented among eligible voters compared with the total population (71 percent versus 63 percent in 2012).

The representation gap for Hispanics and Asians that existed between the total population and eligible voters is even further widened among actual voters. This is because, compared with whites and blacks, fewer Hispanics and Asians who are eligible to vote actually show up at the polls. Because of their recent residence status or lack of information, Hispanics and Asians are less likely to register to vote and to cast ballots. Thus, Hispanics represented only 8 percent of voters in the 2012 presidential election despite constituting more than twice that share of the population. Whites, on the other hand, are far more highly represented among voters than in the population as a whole.

Higher Minority Turnout Impacted the 2008 and 2012 Popular Vote

Although the nation's electorate still lags behind its population with respect to its racial makeup, the minority population made the difference in electing Barack Obama in the 2008 and 2012 presidential elections. A key reason for this was the improved turnout of racial minorities, which magnified their clout among voters.

Minority turnout is important for Democrats in presidential elections. Since the mid-1960s, minorities (as a whole) favored Democrats and whites favored Republicans for president in the national popular vote. The black population has shown the most consistent voting patterns, favoring Democratic presidential candidates since the 1936 second-term election of Franklin D. Roosevelt. While not as strongly favoring Democrats as blacks, Hispanics and Asians also have voted primarily for Democratic candidates in recent elections.

The higher voter turnout of minorities in 2008 and 2012 is shown in Figure B. Black voter turnout increased to a point where nearly two-thirds of black eligible voters cast ballots in 2008 and

2012. Along with the decline in white voter turnout, the 2012 black voter turnout exceeded white voter turnout for the first time since such statistics have been recorded. Although lower than voter turn- out for blacks, Hispanic and Asian turnouts were higher in both Obama elections than in 2004. This higher turnout among all three groups enlarged the size and effect of these voters on the final election outcome.

Obama's two victories followed the 2004 election in which Republican George W. Bush was reelected by 3 million votes—gaining a net of 16 million white votes and losing 13 million minorities. In the subsequent two elections, Obama versus John McCain in 2008 and Obama versus Mitt Romney in 2012, the sizes of minority gains rose to 21 million, and then 23 million votes, respectively. Meanwhile, Republicans showed a decline in

Figure B: Voter Turnout by Race in the 2004, 2008, and 2012 Presidential Elections

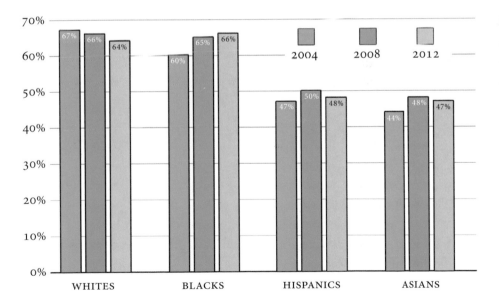

Current Population Survey November 2004, 2008, and 2012 Supplements from William H. Frey, *Diversity Explosion: How New Racial Demographics are Remaking America* (Brookings Institution Press, 2015).

white gains, down to just 12 million in 2008, before registering an insufficient gain of 18 million votes in 2012.

Obama's continued gains in the minority vote were attributable, in part, to the rise in the portion of eligible voters who were minorities. But it was also attributable to higher turnout rates for minorities—increasing their share of all voters—as well as the stronger tendency for these minorities to vote Democratic.[2]

Race and the Nation's Battleground States

The increased minority influence on the popular vote outcomes of the 2008 and 2012 elections were magnified in the Electoral College vote outcomes as the nation's racial demographic shifts dispersed across regions and states. In particular, the Sun Belt region is becoming part of an enlarged battleground of states as minorities become increasingly represented there.

Clearly, racial minorities make up a sizable presence in many states including those not in traditional coastal settlement areas. Minorities constitute nearly one-half or more of the electorates in Hawaii, New Mexico, California, Texas and D.C., and at least one-third or more in a swath of additional states in the South and interior West.

Hispanics embody substantial and increasing portions of the electorates in many Western states as well as Connecticut, Florida, New Jersey, New York and Texas. The Hispanic population may soon approach the black population in electoral clout. Minorities constitute more than one-quarter of the electorate in most Southern states and blacks are the largest group except in Florida, Oklahoma and Texas. Blacks still dominate the small minority populations in whiter heartland states such as Michigan, Ohio and Pennsylvania, though their much smaller Hispanic populations are rising as in other parts of that region.

Although the nation's electorate is still divided somewhat between whiter heartland states and heavily minority coastal states, states in the Sun Belt stand in the forefront of racial electorate change. These include fast-growing Western interior states that are receiving Hispanics and other minorities, and prosperous Southern states that are attracting blacks along with Hispanics from other regions.

The geographic dispersion of new minorities and southward migration of blacks advantage the Democrats by enlarging the number of available battle- ground states. This allowed Democrats to cut into a new electoral turf that Republicans held steadily for a long period, and these trends should pave the way for new state battlegrounds in the future.

In the 2004 election, as in the election four years earlier, George W. Bush won by taking a nearly clean sweep of the interior West and South, along with Great Plains and several Northern states— most notably Ohio—that were then dubbed battlegrounds. This Sun Belt sweep was not new to Republicans. Although they lost some Sun Belt states when Southerner Bill Clinton ran in the three-way elections of 1992 and 1996, and when Southerner Jimmy Carter ran in 1976 and 1980, Republicans held fairly firm control of the South since the Civil Rights years when white Southerners started voting in large numbers for Republican candidates. With very few exceptions, the mostly white conservative-leaning interior West states voted for Republicans continuously from 1968 to 2004, aside from the three-way elections of the 1990s.

The Democratic strongholds for the two elections prior to 2008 consisted of urbanized, racially diverse coastal states such as California and New York and a swath of New England, Northeastern, and Mid- western states with industrial or farming histories. Although these states held constituencies reflecting both new and old strengths of the party—minorities, union workers, progressive professionals and women —they did not represent the most rapidly growing parts of the country.

This geographic map changed with both the 2008 and 2012 elections owing to the changing racial demographics of a number of New Sun Belt states. In contrast to 2004, Obama won new West and South battleground states of Colorado, Florida, Nevada, New Mexico, Virginia and, in 2008, North Carolina.

Table A: States with Largest Voter Representation Gaps, November 2012

MINORITY PERCENT OF

STATE	POPULATION	VOTERS	DIFFERENCE
Arizona	48	28	-20
California	60	43	-17
Texas	58	41	-17
New Mexico	58	43	-15
Nevada	47	33	-14

US Census Current Population Survey, 2012

The effect of the changing demography along with the heightened minority enthusiasm for Obama is illustrated in Nevada. In 2004, Nevada's voters were 80 percent white, 8 percent Hispanic, 6 percent black, and 6 percent Asian or another race. Nevada's white share dropped to 73 percent in 2008 and to 67 percent in 2012 such that, in the latter year, the voters included 15 percent Hispanics, 9 percent blacks, and 9 percent Asians or another race. Aside from demographics alone, the Democratic voting margins (percent voting Democrat minus percent voting Republican) continued to increase particularly for Hispanics from 21 in 2004 to 54 in 2008 and 47 in 2012.

Shifts in this direction were evident in most of the other Sun Belt states that Obama won in 2008, where a rise in the minority Democratic vote overcame the Republican white vote. For most of these South and West battleground states (North Carolina is the exception), Obama's minority support was strong enough to overcome an increased white Republican margin in 2012. This was especially crucial in Florida, where the white Republican margin increased from 14 to 24 between 2008 and 2012. But due to a larger minority turnout and increased Democratic margins, Obama won this key battleground state again.

Racial minorities were responsible for winning five Southern and Western states designated as "battlegrounds" in 2008 (Florida,

Nevada, New Mexico, North Carolina and Virginia) and a similar number in 2012 (excluding North Carolina but including Colorado)—besting the white Republican advantages for these states. This means that the growth of Hispanics, Asians and other new minorities as well as the southward migration of blacks was opening the door to greater future Democratic prospects in the Sun Belt.

Among such states are Arizona and Texas, which are among the five states with the highest minority voter representation gaps, (See Table A) due largely to their substantial and younger Hispanic populations. While both states have voted solidly Republican in past elections, this could change if current race-related Republican and Democratic voting proclivities continue. In these and other states, this representation gap should eventually close— albeit gradually. The "too young to vote" share of the Hispanic population is projected to decrease over time and, as more in the population turn 18, it has been estimated that they will add up to one million new voting-age Hispanic citizens annually for the foreseeable future.[3]

Moreover, the ceiling for greater "new minority" voter participation will increase for two reasons. First, there will be higher rates of naturalization among Hispanic and Asian permanent residents who are eligible to become citizens. Naturalized citizenship rates have increased in recent years, though there is room for further growth. Second, voter turnout rates among Hispanics and Asians, discussed below, will increase as members of these communities become more familiar with registration and voting practices with the help of local government and civic organizations.

It is highly likely that the continued dispersion of minorities to many of the interior Sun Belt states will continue into the future. This would make the longstanding "solid Republican" South and much of the Mountain West become more open to gains by Democrats.[4]

Still, this longer-term prognostication makes some strong assumptions. First, that longstanding white, Republican preferences and minority, Democratic preferences continue into the future. Second, that many of the nation's industrial Midwest states, which will continue to remain "whiter" than the rest of the country, shall remain Democratic.

At least in the short term, the latter assumption may not hold, given that recent Democratic wins were fairly small in Ohio and Pennsylvania, and that Republicans could also be competitive in Iowa and Wisconsin and perhaps Michigan. This is because largely white Republican-leaning baby boomers and seniors could turnout heavily for a popular candidate in these states and could, at least in the short run, counter the growing Democratic-leaning minority populations in the Sun Belt. Still, in the long run, both parties will come to recognize that the larger minority shares of the electorate will not only continue but also need to be reckoned with by adjusting their messages and policy agendas appropriately.

Notes

1. William H. Frey, *Diversity Explosion: How New Racial Demographics are Remaking America* (Brookings Institution Press, 2015).
2. William H. Frey, "Minority Turnout Determined the 2012 Election" (Washington DC: Brookings Institution, May 10, 2013). http://www.brookings.edu/research/papers/2013/05/10-election-2012-minority-voter-turnout-frey.
3. Pew Research Center, "An Awakened Giant: The His panic Electorate Is Likely to Double by 2030." (Washington DC: Pew Hispanic Center, November 14, 2012), p. 7. http:// www.pewhispanic.org/ les/2012/11/hispanic_vote_likely_ to_double_ by_2030_11-14-12.pdf.
4. See William H. Frey, Ruy Teixeira and Robert Griffin, "America's Electoral Future: How Changing Demographics Could Impact Presidential Elections from 2016 to 2032" (Washington DC: Center for American Progress, American Enterprise Institute, Brookings Institution, February 2016). http://www.brookings.edu/~/media/Research/Files/Reports/ 2016/02/25-states-of-change-frey/SOC2016report.pdf?la=en.

> "*It's not only a phenomenon of Phoenix and Dallas and Miami. Iowa, Utah, Nebraska are seeing substantial increases in their minority population, particularly their Hispanic population. And all of these changes are most concentrated and forceful among the young.*"

The "Brown and the Gray" Will Create a Fundamental Political Tension in the Coming Decades

Michele Norris

In the following viewpoint Michele Norris interviews Ron Brownstein, a columnist and editorial director for the National Journal. *Brownstein states that demographic changes are making an impact throughout the country, not simply in the most populous states and major cities. He also offers the view that Democrats have become increasingly dependent on minority voters. This viewpoint should be considered in the context of the times: The interview was conducted during Barack Obama's first term as president and about five years before immigration emerged as one of the most controversial issues in the country. Michele Norris is former host of the NPR news program* All Things Considered.

As you read, consider the following questions:

1. Would you characterize the interviewee to be liberal or conservative in his views about changing demographics and the impact on American politics?
2. How does Brownstein believe aging baby boomers will affect the future of politics in the United States?
3. What is the "brown and gray" phenomenon, according to Brownstein?

M ichele Norris talks with Ron Brownstein of *National Journal* about how the changing US demographics are shifting the political landscape for 2012.

MICHELE NORRIS, host: And those patriotic images evoke an all-American ideal: baseball, picnics, apple pie. We've been thinking about that term all-American, and we're going to spend some time this week exploring what it means at a time when this country's demographics are changing so quickly.

The phrase is often shorthand for a certain idea as in all-American values or a clean-cut all-American boy. In fact, the phrase has its origins in athletics. Back in the 1880s, a sports writer created a hypothetical all-America football team.

Dr. DOUGLAS NOVERR (Michigan State University): These were the best players in all of America.

NORRIS: Douglas Noverr is an American studies professor at Michigan State University. He says the all-America team was supposed to represent the best and the toughest players from around the country.

Dr. NOVERR: You had the celebration of this cult of rugged manliness.

NORRIS: But by the 1930s, Noverr says, there was a new standard bearer.

(Soundbite of radio show, "Jack Armstrong, the All-American Boy")

Unidentified Man #1: Jack Armstrong.

Unidentified Man #2: Jack Armstrong.

Unidentified Man #3: Jack Armstrong.

Unidentified Man #4: Jack Armstrong. The All-American boy.

NORRIS: For the millions who tuned into that popular radio show, the globetrotting boy wonder Jack Armstrong personified...

Dr. NOVERR: Resourcefulness, quick thinking, quest for adventure.

NORRIS: As decades went by, the all-American ideal spread through advertising and entertainment. It was held up as the iconic manifestation of the true American way of life. And underlying all this was a subtle affirmation of the majority culture.

Dr. NOVERR: You also had a very reaffirming, almost comfortable reassurance that this in fact was a Caucasian-dominated term.

NORRIS: But that reassuring term, all-American, is colliding with fast-changing demographics. According to the 2010 census numbers, Asians made the biggest jump in all groups in population growth, and over the next decade, Hispanics are expected to grow to 50 million strong. America is on its way to becoming a majority minority nation.

We asked Ron Brownstein, columnist and editorial director for the *National Journal*, what, if anything, these changes might mean for the 2012 election.

Mr. RON BROWNSTEIN (*National Journal*): America is in the midst of what is probably the most profound demographic change since the turn of the 20th century, and the census report, I think, was like a postcard from the future. It showed that the rate and pace and extent of change was not only deeper and faster than we expected but more widespread.

You know, we think of growing diversity primarily historically we thought of it as a phenomenon of a few big states and a few big cities, and what the census really showed us was that only is the country becoming more diverse than we thought but more places are being affected by it.

It's not only a phenomenon of Phoenix and Dallas and Miami. Iowa, Utah, Nebraska are seeing substantial increases in their minority population, particularly their Hispanic population. And all of these changes are most concentrated and forceful among the young.

Today, the census tells us almost 47 percent of Americans under 18 are minority or non-white. Under 18, our youth population, will be majority minority by the end of this decade. And it kind of begs the question we're going to have to—we may have to come up with some new terminology once we are in that America.

NORRIS: There are a series of gaps in terms of what the census numbers show or indicate and what we actually see in terms of how politics is practiced right now in America, and I want to quickly tick through some of these.

The first is this chiasm between a fast-growing minority—and for now, we'll still use that term—population that will be interested in services and public investment in education, health care, infrastructure, all kinds of things, and then, on the other side, a shrinking and aging white population that doesn't necessarily warm to the idea of using taxes to pay for those investments. Will that chasm continue to grow over time, and what does that mean for public investment?

Mr. BROWNSTEIN: Yeah, I think that is the fundamental political tension that is baked in to our society for the coming decades. I've called this phenomenon the brown and the gray.

You have, as we've said before, an under 18 population, a giant millennial generation that is heavily non-white, soon to be majority non-white, and by and large, those families believe they need public investment, particularly in schools and health care, to help their kids ascend into the middle class.

On the other side, you have a aging baby boom generation that is preponderantly white. Eighty percent of American seniors are white. That proportion isn't going to change much in the coming decades because we essentially cut off immigration into the country between 1924 and 1965. That aging white baby boom has grown increasingly skeptical of government, increasingly resistant to paying taxes to fund government services.

And so you have each political coalition—I mean, this really is the core or the anchor of each political coalition now. The older white population is at the absolute center of the Republican coalition, especially the non-college, working-class part of it. Democrats are increasingly dependent upon the votes of minorities.

About 40 percent of President Obama's vote in 2008 came from minorities, compare to only about 10 percent for John McCain. So you kind of look at these two blocs in the society with very divergent views about the role of government in particular, and you see this conflict, I think, playing out not only nationally but in states.

I think a lot of what we've seen in Arizona, in Texas, in Florida, these are states where there are the biggest gaps between the demography of the under-18 population and the over-65 population, what Bill Frey, a demographer at Brookings Institution, has called the cultural generation gap.

NORRIS: The demographic shifts that we've been talking about, how did that play out in terms of the sort of coded language of American politics when people talk about things like Joe Sixpack or, you know, taking the country back or what it means to be all-American?

Mr. BROWNSTEIN: Well, I have felt, until recently, that in general, American politics today was less racialized than it was in the '70s and '80s. There were a series of very racially overt issues—affirmative action, bussing, crime, welfare—that really served to polarize the country along racial lines and lead to this realignment.

But in the '90s, under Bill Clinton, the welfare issue was largely taken off the table. The mend-it-don't-end-it reduced the toxicity of affirmative action as an issue. And crime went down nationally. George W. Bush did not really play in these waters, either. And so I kind of felt that, you know, roughly from say '92, post-Willie Horton, to 2008, we were in a less I think racially incendiary or explosive kind of political environment.

I think that is beginning to change again. It is moving or transmuting into this debate about the role of government, and I think many of these debates are now re-acquiring a kind of racial content to them, even if there is no racial language.

And I can point to one empirical fact on that. You know, we do a quarterly poll here called—at National Journal called the Heartland Monitor. The last one, we looked at how Americans feel about the changing diversity. And there is no question that whites who say they are troubled by the pace of racial change express conservative views on a whole series of other issues, particularly the role of government.

These kind of perspectives are intertwined and are interconnected, I think, to a degree we haven't seen since the 1980s. I think we are seeing attitudes about race and broader ideological attitudes kind of reconnecting in a potentially powerful way.

NORRIS: Ronald Brownstein is editorial director and a columnist for the *National Journal.* Ron, thanks so much for making time for us.

Mr. BROWNSTEIN: Thank you.

NORRIS: Tomorrow we continue our conversations about what it means to be all-American in light of the country's changing demographics. We hear from Asian-Americans trying to break what's known as the bamboo ceiling in corporate America.

Unidentified Woman: In an organization, you do need to understand how to promote yourself to get ahead. And I think if you talk to most of the Asian individuals who are working in these organizations, most of them are uncomfortable with that because they didn't grow up with that as something that was valued.

NORRIS: That's tomorrow in our series that explores the evolving term all-American.

> *"If the media and others covered third parties more, unaligned voters—for example, people who believe in peace and freedom—would have a new incentive to participate and give a positive vote."*

Voting Third Party Will Have More of an Impact

Stephen Weese

In the following viewpoint Stephen Weese argues that, based on a number of factors, Americans should strongly consider voting for third party candidates. The author notes that polarization between the two major political parties has increased to historic levels. As well, polls showed very negative ratings for the 2016 Republican and Democrat presidential candidates. The author contends that most voters actually fall in the middle, yet they are forced to choose a candidate more extreme than they'd like. Third parties are the answer, Weese contends, and the emergence of social media and an open-minded younger generation of voters are likely to make third party candidates more viable in future elections. Stephen Weese has a master's degree in Computer Information Technology from Regis University. He teaches college math and computer courses.

As you read, consider the following questions:

1. What is First Pass the Post voting?
2. To what extent have partisan politics become more extreme over the past decade?
3. How can new media help the emergence of viable third party candidates, according to the viewpoint?

I magine living in a world where there are only two choices. Chocolate or vanilla. Hot or cold. Light or darkness. There are no in-betweens. No "shades of gray." You must explain everything as a "yes or no" dichotomy. On or off. False or true. This binary reality leaves little room for human diversity or creativity—yet it is in this exact reality we find ourselves trapped with the US political system.

Prelude to Deception

It all starts with a sociological phenomenon created due to our political election process. First Past the Post means that in our elections, winner takes all and the loser gets nothing. We are told that if we do not vote for one of the two major parties, our vote is wasted. (I mathematically analyzed this myth in a previous article.)

The concept that underlies the two party phenomenon is not only mathematical in principle, it is sociological. Duverger's law assumes that people faced with more than two choices in a First Past the Post election will vote against the most radical or undesired opponent, instead of for the candidate they most desire. This demonstrates what is called a "negative" vote—it could be more precisely described as a vote made out of fear of the worst candidate.

Another principle of Duverger's law is that it filters out "weaker" parties in that people will not vote for a party that has no chance of winning. This weakness is only psychologically defined; a party could appear weaker simply due to less publicity. Certainly a third party could have better ideas than the main two—but if the ideas are not heard, then no one can know about them. The purely cognitive illusion that there are only two "worthy" parties is perpetuated by lack of media coverage and the false appeal to common practice that it's the "way things always have been done."

The simple truth is, Duverger's law depends on the psychological basis of fear and ignorance. Without these factors in society, the mathematical differences would disappear.

The Two Major Parties are Weak

At this point, the two major candidates for election, Donald Trump and Hillary Clinton, have historically high negative numbers. In fact, the two frontrunners have the highest unfavorable ratings since those numbers have been tracked: Trump is net negative 33, and Clinton negative 21.

More voters see these candidates in an unfavorable light than a favorable one. This would be a perfect time for the rise of a third party, even according to Duverger's law. It only takes a cursory look at the news to see the large anti-Trump movement among major Republicans as well as the staunch Sanders wing of the Democratic party. The parties are divided and their candidates are weak, as shown by the polls above.

The Electorate Is Polarized

If you have the feeling that in the last decade partisan politics has become more extreme and vitriolic you'd be correct—Pew research has been tracking this phenomenon. Both the extremity of Democratic and Republican views have increased, as well as dislike and intolerance for the "other" party. At this point, 92% of Republicans are to the right of the median Democrat, and 94% of Democrats are to the left of the median Republican.

There are double the amount of pure liberals and conservatives than a decade ago, and the fear of the opposing party has doubled as well. Twice as many people think that the alternate party threatens the "nation's well-being."

This polarization affects people's choices of where to live, shop, and travel, and even goes to the extent of opposition to a family member marrying someone of the opposing party. The Pew study also shows that those on the extreme ends of the spectrum are the most politically active—writing letters, posting on social media, travelling to political events (though this is hardly surprising.) The effect of this of course is that these parties are represented more by their extreme elements.

This polarization also results in one-dimensional thinking. People only think of politics as "right" or "left" because this is all they have ever known. As humans, are we only one-dimensional? Aren't there more ways to look at solving the problems of a nation than just left and right?

Most of us are trapped in this one-dimensional illusory world, like a train stuck on a single track. The mere idea that we could travel in a completely different direction is a foreign concept. Even a middle-school student can tell you that we live in a world with three dimensions, that we can travel in an infinite variety of paths. Yet we find ourselves confined to this oversimplified model of reality that goes counter to our interests and only allows us choices that leave most dissatisfied.

Majority in the Middle

Another effect of this polarization is that moderate Americans find themselves in the middle of this extremism. Most voters do not view the other party as a threat to the nation and are not 100% liberal or conservative in their views. There are actually more people in the middle, yet they find themselves forced to choose to side with one extreme or the other. In 2014, the "mixed" electorate (holding views from both sides) was 39%.

There are less of them now, due to extremism, yet this 39% in the middle is enough to completely take over an election, if they only had a different option to choose from. Unfortunately, the Pew data also shows that the people in the middle are less likely to vote and participate in the election process. Duverger's law is working here because these moderates do not know that they are a huge bloc that could elect a moderate candidate with ease.

Overcoming Ignorance and Fear

As we have seen, voting tendencies in our system are predicated on fear of a radical candidate as well as ignorance of third party platforms or even their existence. This is the one-dimensional illusion we live in. If we continue to be more polarized, more and more of the electorate will hate the other half.

If nothing stops this progress, those in the middle will be forced to choose a side as the tolerance for opposing views decreases. Others could stand up and speak and become a driving force pulling opinions back toward some sense of centrism—or even better, they could propose ideas outside of the traditional "left vs. right" paradigm.

The truth is, if people could overcome the fear of the "worst" candidate and voted for what they believed in, the facade would begin to crumble. If the media and others covered third parties more, unaligned voters—for example, people who believe in peace and freedom—would have a new incentive to participate and give a positive vote.

Fortunately, we now live in the age of new media—a social movement can begin online without the backing of a major television or news network. This election is the most opportune time for this to happen given the record negative views of both candidates. Thus it behooves the unaligned voter to find her or his voice in this election. If these voters together decided that "enough is enough" and realized that they are actually the most powerful voting bloc, they could simply say "no" to the two major parties—and nothing could stop them.

> *"Such was the distance he moved the political dial in Texas—his was the best showing by a Democrat in a US Senate race for 20 years—he is certain to have a prominent voice in the party from now on. He took a state that had been written off by progressives for decades, and virtually single-handedly wrestled it into play."*

Demographic Shifts Are Changing Election Outcomes

Ed Pilkington and Tom Dart

In the following viewpoint Ed Pilkington and Tom Dart argue that the narrownesss of Beto O'Rourke's defeat by incumbent Ted Cruz in the 2018 midterm Senate election spotlighted a shift among young voters, even in Texas, as well as an influx of Hispanic immigrants fighting back against the immigration views and policies of Donald Trump, toward greater liberalism. The authors state that the close election in a conservative state provides hope for Democrats that the huge number of electoral votes in Texas can be won by the right candidate. Ed Pilkington is chief reporter for Guardian US. He is the author of Beyond the Mother Country. *Tom Dart is a freelance journalist based in Houston, Texas.*

"Beto O'Rourke 'As Hopeful as I've Ever Been' Despite Narrow Loss to Ted Cruz," by Ed Pilkington and Tom Dart, Guardian News and Media Limited, November 7, 2018. Reprinted by permission.

As you read, consider the following questions:

1. Based on this article, what was the appeal of Beto O'Rourke to young voters in Texas?
2. O'Rourke has been criticized for lacking policy ideas. Do you agree with that assessment after reading this piece?
3. What reasons does Beto O'Rourke give for being hopeful despite his defeat to Ted Cruz?

In the end, the night was not to be his. Beto O'Rourke, an obscure Democratic member of Congress from the border town of El Paso who has risen to be one of his party's new superstars, conceded defeat in his insurgent bid to unseat Ted Cruz from a US Senate seat in Texas—but in words that sounded like those of the victor.

"I believe in you, I believe in Texas and I believe in this country," he told a crowd in his home town of El Paso. "I'm as inspired, I'm as hopeful as I've ever been in my life. Tonight's loss does nothing to diminish the way that I feel about Texas or this country."

Thousands of O'Rourke supporters had waited hours for their champion to appear, filling a baseball stadium. Though the mood grew sombre when news came in of his defeat, it lit up when he took to the stage shortly after 10pm with chants of "Beto! Beto!" rising above the crowd.

Long before election day O'Rourke was being compared with Robert Kennedy for his charisma, good looks, rhetorical skills and intense political passions.

Such was the distance he moved the political dial in Texas— his was the best showing by a Democrat in a US Senate race for 20 years—he is certain to have a prominent voice in the party from now on. He took a state that had been written off by progressives for decades, and virtually single-handedly wrestled it into play.

"O'Rourke raised more money than any other Texas Democrat, electrified crowds like no Texas Democrat (or Republican) in recent history, and breathed new life into a moribund Democratic party. While Beto-mania has bitten the dust tonight, he still has a bright future ahead of him," said Mark Jones, a political scientist at Rice University.

Julian Castro, Obama's housing secretary and the former mayor of San Antonio, told the Guardian that by coming so close, O'Rourke had given a major boost to Democratic hopes in Texas. "His achievement is to show that Texas, with its 38 electoral college votes in presidential elections, is back in play."

Castro added: "This is a wake-up call for this state. Democrats can go much further and faster than anyone had thought."

Ted Cruz celebrated hanging on to his Senate seat in front of several hundred supporters had gathered in a hotel ballroom in one of Houston's swankiest districts.

When Cruz entered the ballroom he high-fived his fans as they chanted "U-S-A!" and embraced his wife, Heidi, before taking the stage. "Texans came together behind a commonsense agenda of low taxes, low regulations and lots and lots of jobs. Securing the border and keeping our communities safe and defending the constitution and the Bill of Rights," he said.

The 47-year-old also called for more civility, respect and dignity in politics, which sounded a touch hollow from a man who only two weeks earlier had appeared on stage at a rally held by Donald Trump in Cruz's honour in which the president deployed his usual repertoire of ultra-partisan insults and false claims.

Cruz—Trump's sworn enemy when they fought for the 2016 Republican presidential nomination—genuflected before him and ran a campaign based almost entirely on turning out a base of white, conservative Trump loyalists.

As the battle heated up, Cruz, relying on suburban and rural voters, relentlessly attacked his Democratic opponent as too liberal for Texas, portraying him as far-left Hollywood celebrity bait, a Bernie Sanders-style socialist out of touch with traditional values—that is to say, a full-throated embrace of God, guns, fossil fuels, low taxes and limited government.

Cruz hammered O'Rourke on his pro-immigration policies, warning of the dire consequences of allowing "caravans" of

How Immigration May Have Decided the 2016 Presidential Election

Immigration is already a top issue in the 2016 presidential race, as it was in previous election cycles. In 2012, harsh rhetoric dramatically affected the Republican Party's appeal with Hispanic and Asian voters—they lost over 70 percent of that vote in the presidential race—and among other immigrant-friendly voting blocs. Looking toward the 2016 election, factors such as shifting demographics and voter attitudes have increased the impact that a candidate's position on the issue will have on his or her ultimate success at the ballot box.

Poll Says Anti-Immigration Stance Is a Mistake for GOP Candidates

In June, the Partnership joined Romney 2012 Deputy Campaign Manager Katie Packer Gage and Burning Glass Consulting in conducting polling and focus groups of GOP likely caucus goers in Iowa, likely GOP primary voters in both New Hampshire and South Carolina, and likely general election voters in ten swing states.

The findings are clear: the benefits to being viewed as anti-immigration in a Republican primary are small, while the costs of doing so in the general election are extremely large.

Check out the *Washington Post*'s coverage, "How immigration could cripple the Republican nominee long before the 2016 election," (http://www.washingtonpost.com/blogs/the-fix/wp/2015/06/17/how-

Central American asylum seekers into the country in an echo of Trump. He also turned into an attack ad a viral video in which the Democrat said there was "nothing more American" than kneeling during the national anthem as NFL players had done in protest at police brutality.

Nonetheless, when the result was certain and O'Rourke posed no more threat, Cruz took time to congratulate his opponent. O'Rourke, he said, had "poured his heart into this campaign, he worked tirelessly, he's a dad and he took time away from his kids.

immigration-could-cripple-the-republican-nominee-long-before-the-2016-general-election/) or read the findings for yourself here.

- Candidates perceived as anti-immigration will start the general election at a 24-point disadvantage among likely voters and at an even greater disadvantage among key electoral groups, like college-educated white women, young voters, and Hispanics—the very groups who will determine which party takes the White House.
- In the primaries, only about one in five GOP primary voters is an anti-immigration voter. This pool is not only small, but comprises hardline voters who are virtually unwinnable for any mainstream candidate. In other words, the benefits of being perceived as anti-immigration in the primaries are minimal, but the costs in the general election are huge.

Katie Packer Gage reflects on the 2012 Romney experience in a *Politico Magazine* piece: "I saw first-hand how the rhetoric on immigration during the GOP primary, from all of the candidates, painted our party in a negative light and came back to bite us in the general election." Read the piece: "Don't Repeat Mitt Romney's Mistake on Immigration" (http://www.politico.com/magazine/story/2015/06/dont-repeat-mitt-romneys-mistake-on-immigration-119087.html#.VZFsi-1Viko).

Governor Romney himself reflected on his experience in 2012 and acknowledged, "I think the biggest mistake I made was not focusing very early on minority voters."

"Why Immigration May Decide the 2016 Election," New American Economy.

Let me say to all of those who worked on his campaign, those who were inspired, that I am your senator as well and my responsibility is to represent every Texan."

Before Cruz gave his victory speech in Houston, his father Raphael appeared on stage. "The message is loud and clear," he told the Republican crowd. "Texas remains solid red!"

But that message is not at all clear after a bruising campaign that saw the Democratic underdog come far too close to winning the Senate seat for comfort. The last time a Democrat successfully did that was in 1994.

O'Rourke began his David versus Goliath mission to topple Cruz less than two years ago with a staff of just two—both old friends from El Paso—travelling in a rented sedan. He started from scratch in a state with next to no Democratic party infrastructure, criss-crossing the state to stump in all of its 254 counties—no small task in Texas, which is bigger than France.

Wherever he went, he planted seeds of a new Democratic infrastructure—something that has been sorely lacking in Texas since the 1990s. They began recruiting volunteers, often young and inexperienced but energetic and eager, who grew into an army by election day, numbering 25,000.

O'Rourke's team created 727 "pop-up" offices, converting volunteers' homes into hubs of activity. By the end they had knocked on almost 2m doors.

The Democratic candidate went to extreme lengths to mobilise every potential vote. When the Guardian reported on an Hispanic young man in Gonzalez that had never voted and had no intention of starting now, he dispatched his field officer from 70 miles away to register the individual and encourage him to cast his ballot.

Financially, he also tore up the traditional rulebook. He refused from the beginning to accept money from big donors or political action committees, preferring instead to rely on the beneficence of his passionate supporters.

The gamble worked—O'Rourke smashed previous US Senate fundraising records, hugely outgunning Cruz by drawing in about $70m from more than 1m small online donations to his opponent's $30m.

In the end, the vastly superior ground game that the Republican party has built up over many years was simply too much for one individual politician to overcome.

But the narrow result still represents a stark improvement for the Democrats in Texas, a state that turned majority minority in 2004 and with its rapidly growing population holds enormous weight in US electoral politics. Were the Democrats able to win Texas in presidential races they would effectively banish the Republicans from the White House.

Perhaps O'Rourke's most important achievement has been to prove that groups that have been written off as potential voters in Texas—notably young people aged 19 to 29—can be brought to electoral life. His campaign led to a surge of voter registration that added 1.6 million voters to Texas voter rolls.

Having registered them, O'Rourke's army of volunteers then persuaded them to actually go to the polling stations, leading to a massive surge of early voting that saw almost 5 million Texans vote early—more than the total who cast ballots in the last midterm elections in 2014.

Cynthia Valdez, a customer service assistant in El Paso, is one of the new legions of Democratic voters in Texas unleashed by O'Rourke. She is 27, but voted for the first time in early voting last month.

She said she was partly motivated by Trump. "He is not for the people, he is only interested in himself, his friends and the rich. He only cares about money."

And it was partly motivated by O'Rourke. "He's for the average person. He cares about us."

> *"Republicans know that their base*
> *of older white Christians is the*
> *most rapidly shrinking part of the*
> *electorate. They cannot manufacture*
> *more of these voters, but they*
> *can restrict turnout by the rising*
> *Democratic base of minorities and*
> *young people."*

What Motivates Voters May Be Changing

Allan J. Lichtman

In the following viewpoint Allan J. Lichtman argues that the 2018 midterm elections would prove to be a referendum on the presidency of Donald Trump. His words proved prophetic when the Democrats made significant gains in Congress and took over the House of Representatives by a wide margin. Lichtman writes about how demographic shifts in states with gubernatorial, House, and Senate races seemed to favor Democrats. And though Republicans won some of those elections, including hotly contested races for governor in Florida and Georgia, the gains made by Democrats overall were the result at least partially of liberal shifts among young voters and a growing number of minorities. Allan J. Lichtman is distinguished professor of history at American University in Washington, DC.

As you read, consider the following questions:

1. Based on the viewpoint, were the 2016 midterm election results a referendum on voters' feelings about Donald Trump?
2. What did the results of the 2016 midterms say about the future of the American electorate?
3. Why did some believe the 2016 election was the most important midterm balloting in American history, according to the viewpoint?

Donald Trump was right when he said that America's midterm elections will be about him. Midterm elections are always to some degree a referendum on the incumbent president, and Trump is the most polarizing president in the modern history of the United States. He has inspired a fervent following and an equally passionate opposition. The midterm results will depend on what drives more turnout this year—love or hate of Trump.

For Trump's backers, he is a true populist who has toppled a crooked political establishment that pursued its own interests at the expense of ordinary Americans. He created a booming economy, cut taxes, unshackled enterprise from stifling regulations, and renegotiated the job-killing North American Trade Agreement (Nafta). He has protected the nation from Islamic terrorists and traditional American culture from corrupting foreign influences. He has exposed the bias of the mainstream media and backed religious freedom for Christians. Trump has appointed reliable conservatives to the supreme court and stood against the baby-killing abortion industry.

For detractors, Trump is a phony populist whose policies have benefited the rich and imposed a crushing burden of debt on the American people. By rolling back environmental regulations and withdrawing from the Paris climate accord, he has exposed Americans to the ravages of catastrophic climate change. He has diminished America's international standing, and instead of championing democracy and human rights, he has cultivated some of world's most brutal dictators.

Trump has lied repeatedly to the American people, demeaned women and minorities, undermined the free press, condoned violence against his enemies, and attacked migrants and refugees as murderers and rapists. For his most ardent critics, Trump has destroyed civility and created a toxic environment that contributed to Robert Bowers' massacre of congregants at the Tree of Life synagogue and Cesar Sayoc's dispatching of bombs to CNN and critics of Trump.

Two-thirds of respondents to an NPR/PBS NewsHour/Marist poll taken in late October said that Trump will be a factor in their midterm votes; 23% said that he will be a minor factor; 44% said he will be a major factor. A similar poll taken before the midterm elections of 2014 found that then president Barack Obama would be either a minor or a major factor in voting for only 47% of respondents.

"This is definitively a national election," Lee Miringoff, director of the Marist Institute for Public Opinion, said. "With a referendum on Trump."

Voter turnout is typically low in midterm elections, falling well below participation in parliamentary elections in other advanced democracies. Only about 38% of US citizens voted in the 2014 midterms, leaving some 140m votes on the table.

But Trump will likely inspire higher turnout this year. He "has attracted passionate loyalty, and passionate antagonism, and hatred and love tend to drive people to the polls," Henry Olsen, a senior fellow at the Democracy Fund Voter Study Group, said. "We'll probably see a much higher than normal turnout for the midterms."

Unlike the past two midterm elections, polls indicate that this year Democrats have equaled or gained the edge on Republicans in voter enthusiasm. A Gallup Poll conducted from mid- to late-October found that "Democrats match or exceed Republicans on turnout indicators." Republicans have countered with voter suppression efforts.

Republicans know that their base of older white Christians is the most rapidly shrinking part of the electorate. They cannot manufacture more of these voters, but they can restrict turnout by the rising Democratic base of minorities and young people through purges of registration rolls, stringent voter ID laws, poll closings and exact-match laws that suspend voters' registration for the smallest mismatch between information on the registration forms and driver's licenses or social security records.

In Georgia, relying on a 2017 exact-match law passed by the Republican legislature, Brian Kemp, the Republican secretary of state who is also running for governor, suspended some 53,000 registrations. Minorities accounted for some 80% of suspended registrations.

In North Dakota, after Democrat Heidi Heitkamp was elected senator by 3,000 votes in 2012, the Republican legislature required proof of a street address as a prerequisite for voting. The law placed a disparate burden on the Democratic base of Native American voters, who often live on unnamed roads and depend upon post office boxes for the delivery of mail.

Yet, voting restrictions may backfire on Republicans by motivating opposition voters. In North Dakota, Mark Trahant, editor of Indian Country Today, said that in the past "the Native vote has not necessarily turned out … but with tribes working overtime to help members obtain valid addresses and ID, she [Heitkamp] actually could get a turnout of Native voters she wouldn't have gotten any other way."

In Georgia, Kemp's Democratic opponent, Stacey Abrams, an African American woman, has urged supporters to flood the polls to fight "voter suppression". In a leaked audio recording, Kemp confidentially warned supporters about "the literally tens of millions of dollars that they"—his opponents—"are putting behind the get out and vote efforts for their base."

Kemp was especially concerned about absentee ballots, and what would happen "if everybody uses and exercises their right to vote, which they absolutely can, and mails those ballots in."

> *"At its core, demography is the act of counting people. But it's also important to study the forces that are driving population change, and measure how these changes have an impact on people's lives."*

America and the World Are Changing Drastically

D'Vera Cohn and Andrea Caumont

In the following viewpoint D'Vera Cohn and Andrea Caumont examine demographic trends, many of which have affected the United States politically, socially, and economically. Among them are a growing number of minorities, including immigrants, changes in family structure, and an ever-increasing number of women in the workforce. The authors also cite a shrinking link to religious beliefs among younger Americans. D'Vera Cohn is a senior writer and editor at Pew Research Center. She studies and writes about demographics in the United States. Andrea Caumont is social media editor at Pew Research Center.

"10 Demographic Trends That Are Shaping the U.S. and the World," by D'Vera Cohn and Andrea Caumont, Pew Research Center, Washington, DC, March 31, 2016. http://www.pewresearch.org/fact-tank/2016/03/31/10-demographic-trends-that-are-shaping-the-u-s-and-the-world/. Used in accordance with Pew Research Center reuse Policy. http://www.pewresearch.org/terms-and-conditions/. Usage in no way implies endorsement.

As you read, consider the following questions:

1. Which demographic trends do you believe will have the greatest impact on the United States in the future?
2. What is the new generation to watch, according to the viewpoint?
3. How has the recent role of women in the workforce changed America, according to this viewpoint?

At its core, demography is the act of counting people. But it's also important to study the forces that are driving population change, and measure how these changes have an impact on people's lives. For example, how does immigration affect US population growth? Do Americans feel that children are better off with a parent at home, in an era when most women work? How is the rise of the young-adult Millennial generation contributing to the rise of Americans with no stated religion? For this year's Population Association of America (PAA) annual meeting, here is a roundup of some of Pew Research Center's recent demography-related findings that tell us how America and the world are changing.

1. Americans Are More Racially and Ethnically Diverse Than in the Past, and the US Is Projected to Be Even More Diverse in the Coming Decades

By 2055, the US will not have a single racial or ethnic majority. Much of this change has been (and will be) driven by immigration. Nearly 59 million immigrants have arrived in the US in the past 50 years, mostly from Latin America and Asia. Today, a near-record 14% of the country's population is foreign born compared with just 5% in 1965. Over the next five decades, the majority of US population growth is projected to be linked to new Asian and Hispanic immigration. American attitudes about immigration and diversity are supportive of these changes for the most part. More Americans say immigrants strengthen the country than say they burden it, and most say the US's increasing ethnic diversity makes it a better place to live.

2. Asia Has Replaced Latin America (Including Mexico) as the Biggest Source of New Immigrants to the US

In a reversal of one of the largest mass migrations in modern history, net migration flows from Mexico to the US turned negative between 2009 and 2014, as more Mexicans went home than arrived in the US. And after rising steadily since 1990, the unauthorized immigrant population has leveled off in recent years, falling to 11.3 million in 2014 from a high of 12.2 million in 2007. Meanwhile, Asians are now the only major racial or ethnic group whose numbers are rising mainly because of immigration. And while African immigrants make up a small share of the US immigrant population, their numbers are also growing steadily— roughly doubling every decade since 1970.

3. America's Demographic Changes Are Shifting the Electorate—and American Politics

The 2016 electorate will be the most diverse in US history due to strong growth among Hispanic eligible voters, particularly US-born youth. There are also wide gaps opening up between the generations on many social and political issues. Young adult Millennials are much more likely than their elders to hold liberal views on many political and social issues, though they are also less likely to identify with either political party: 50% call themselves political independents.

4. Millennials, Young Adults Born from 1981 to 1996, Are the New Generation to Watch

By 2019 they will surpass Baby Boomers (born 1946-1964) as the largest US adult generation, and they differ significantly from their elders in many ways. They are the most racially diverse adult generation in American history: 43% of Millennials are nonwhite, the highest share of any generation. And while they are on track to be the most educated generation to date, this achievement has come at a cost: Many Millennials are struggling with student debt. In addition to the weak labor market of recent years, student debt is perhaps one reason why many are still living at home. Despite these troubles, Millennials are the most upbeat about their financial future: More than eight-in-ten say they either currently have enough money to lead the lives they want or expect to in the future.

5. Women's Role in the Labor Force and Leadership Positions Has Grown Dramatically

The labor force participation rate for American women has risen steadily since the 1960s. In fact, mothers were the sole or primary breadwinner in a record 40% of all households with children in 2011. The gender pay gap has narrowed over this period of time, especially for young women just entering the labor force, but it still persists. As more women have entered the workforce, the share of women in top leadership jobs has risen, but they still make up a small share of the nation's political and business leaders relative to men. Why the continued disparity? While Americans say women are every bit as capable of being good leaders as men, four-in-ten believe they are held to higher standards than men and that the US is just not ready to put more women in top leadership positions.

6. The American Family Is Changing

After decades of declining marriage rates, the share of american adults who have never been married is at an historic high. Two-parent households are on the decline in the U.S., while divorce, remarriage and cohabitation are on the rise. About one-in-six American kids now live in a blended family. And the roles of mothers and fathers are converging, due in part to the rise of breadwinner moms. Dads are doing more housework and child care, while moms are doing more paid work outside the home. Americans are conflicted about some aspects of this change: While nearly half of two-parent households have a mom and dad who both work full time, 51% of Americans say children are better off with a mother at home.

7. The Share of Americans Who Live in Middle Class Households Is Shrinking

The share of US adults living in middle-income households fell to 50% in 2015, after more than four decades in which those households served as the nation's economic majority. And the financial gaps between middle- and upper-income Americans have widened, with upper-income households holding 49% of US aggregate household income (up from 29% in 1970) and seven times as much wealth as middle-income households (up from three times as much in 1983). Most Americans say the government doesn't do enough to help the middle class, and neither political party is widely viewed as a champion for middle-class interests.

8. Christians Are Declining as a Share of the US Population, and the Number of US Adults Who Do Not Identify With Any Organized Religion Has Grown

While the US remains home to more Christians than any other country, the percentage of Americans identifying as Christian dropped from 78% in 2007 to 71% in 2014. By contrast, the religiously unaffiliated have surged seven percentage points in that time span to make up 23% of US adults last year. This trend has been driven in large part by Millennials, 35% of whom are religious "nones." The rise of the "nones" is not a story unique to the US: The unaffiliated are now the second-largest religious group in 48% of the world's nations. Americans are well aware of this shift: 72% say religion's influence on public life is waning, and most who say this see it as a bad thing.

9. The World's Religious Makeup Will Look a Lot Different by 2050

Over the next four decades, Christians will remain the largest religious group, but Islam will grow faster than any other major religion, mostly because Muslims are younger and have more children than any other religious group globally. By 2050, the number of Muslims will nearly equal the number of Christians. In the US, the Muslim population will remain small, but is projected to grow rapidly.

10. The World Is Aging

The demographic future for the US and the world looks very different than the recent past. Growth from 1950 to 2010 was rapid—the global population nearly tripled, and the US population doubled. However, population growth from 2010 to 2050 is projected to be significantly slower and is expected to tilt strongly to the oldest age groups, both globally and in the US. Public opinion on whether the growing number of older people is a problem varies dramatically around the world. Concern is highest in East Asia where large majorities describe aging as a major problem for their countries.

Periodical and Internet Sources Bibliography

The following articles have been selected to supplement the diverse views presented in this chapter.

Perry Bacon Jr. and Dhrumil Mehta, "Republicans and Democrats Should Be Worried about 2020," Five Thirty Eight, April 20, 2018. https://fivethirtyeight.com/features/republicans-_and_-democrats-should-be-worried-about-2020/.

Marc Caputo, Steven Shepard, and Scott Bland, "Population Boom Could Remake 2020 Map," Politico, December 19, 2018. https://www.politico.com/story/2018/12/19/population-boom-could-remake-2020-map-1070784.

Dante Chinni, "Demographic Shifts Show 2020 Presidential Race Could Be Close," NBC News, April 22, 2018. https://www.nbcnews.com/politics/first-read/demographic-shifts-show-2020-presidential-race-could-be-close-n868146.

John Della Volpe, "Midterms Saw Historic Turnout by Young Voters," Real Clear Politics, November 8, 2018. https://www.realclearpolitics.com/articles/2018/11/08/midterms_saw_historic_turnout_by_young_voters__138591.html.

Lloyd Green, "It's the Demographics, Stupid: Party Loyalties Are Shifting as 2020 Looms," The *Guardian*, December 22, 2018. https://www.theguardian.com/us-news/2018/dec/22/2020-election-republican-democrat-demographics-party-loyalties.

Rob Griffin, Ruy Teixeira, and William Frey, "America's Electoral Future: Demographic Shifts and the Future of the Trump Coalition," Center for American Progress, April 14, 2018. https://www.americanprogress.org/issues/democracy/reports/2018/04/14/449461/americas-electoral-future-2/.

Ramon Taylor, "Will Changing Demographics Shift Voting Patterns?" VOA, November 1, 2018. https://www.voanews.com/usa/us-politics/will-changing-demographics-shift-voting-patterns.

Jason VanAlstine, Steven R. Cox, and Dianne M. Roden, "Cultural Diversity in the United States and Its Impact on Human Development," *Journal of the Indiana Academy of the Social Sciences*, 2015. https://digitalcommons.butler.edu/cgi/viewcontent.cgi?article=1027&context=jiass.

For Further Discussion

Chapter 1

1. How will future demographics affect the gun control debate?
2. Will global warming grow into the most important issue among young Americans in the future?
3. How will the political power gained by millennials and Generation Xers affect LGBTQ rights in the future?

Chapter 2

1. Is the current health care system properly set up to handle the huge number of baby boomers reaching old age?
2. Does the United States have too large a population to handle a Medicare for All system affordably?
3. How can Americans show greater appreciation for the elderly?

Chapter 3

1. Do you foresee more or less welcoming attitudes and policies toward Latino immigrants in the future?
2. Will Americans be more or less nationalistic after Donald Trump's presidency has ended?
3. Are free tuition and wiping out all current college debt through legislation realistic and viable possibilities?

Chapter 4

1. How will demographic shifts change the electoral map in the future?
2. Which current demographic trend is having the biggest impact?
3. Will today's young voters grow more conservatively as they age?

Organizations to Contact

The editors have compiled the following list of organizations concerned with the issues debated in this book. The descriptions are derived from materials provided by the organizations. All have publications or information available for interested readers. The list was compiled on the date of publication of the present volume; the information provided here may change. Be aware that many organizations take several weeks or longer to respond to inquiries, so allow as much time as possible.

Alliance for Climate Education

4696 Broadway, Suite 2
Boulder, CO 80304
(720) 383-7129
website: https://acespace.org

Alliance for Climate Education seeks to educate high school students about climate change. It takes steps to empower young people to work toward positive solutions.

American Civil Liberties Union (ACLU)

125 Broad Street
18th floor
New York, NY 10004
(212) 549-2500
email: aclupreferences@aclu.org
website: www.aclu.org

The American Civil Liberties Union uses its resources to fight for and preserve individual rights and freedoms in the United States.

Center for American Progress

1333 H Street NW
10th Floor
Washington, DC 20005
(202) 682-1611
website: www.americanprogress.org

The Center of American Progress seeks to improve the lives of all Americans through bold, progressive ideas and concerted action.

Democracy Matters

201 Riverview Drive
Poughkeepsie, NY 12601-3935
(315) 725-4211
email: www.democracymatters.org/contact-democracy-matters
website: www.democracymatters.org

Democracy Matters helps students organize projects connecting pro-democracy reforms on such issues as the environment, civil rights, education, and health care. Its goal is to reduce the role of money and increase the role of activists into the American political system.

Federal Election Commission

1050 First Street NE
Washington, DC 20463
(800) 424-9530
website: www.fec.gov

This independent government agency regulates, administrates, and enforces federal campaign finance law. It oversees the financing of campaigns for the House of Representatives, Senate, presidency, and vice presidency.

Hip Hop Congress

50 Woodside Road, #203
Redwood City, CA 94061
(213) 215-5257
email: hiphopcongressinc@gmail.com
website: www.hiphopcongress.com

Hip Hop Congress is a network of individuals and organizations seeking to change the world by uplifting culture for the creative development of artists and young people. The organization works to achieve its goals through education, civic engagement, and equitable resource exchange.

Independent Voter Project

PO Box 34431
San Diego, CA 92163
(619) 207-4618
website: www.independentvoterproject.org

The IVP is a nonprofit, nonpartisan group seeking to better inform voters about important public policy issues and to encourage nonpartisan voters to participate in the electoral process.

New America

740 15th Street NW, Suite 900
Washington, DC 20005
(202) 986-2700
website: https://www.newamerica.org/political-reform

The political reform program of New America, which began in 2014, looks to launch new strategies and innovations to repair what it perceives as the dysfunction of government, restore citizen trust, and rebuild the promise of American democracy.

Political Media

1750 Tysons Boulevard, Suite 1500
McLean, VA, 22102
(202) 558-6640
website: http://politicalmedia.com

The mission of Political Media is to clearly and strongly espouse the benefits of the rights and responsibilities of liberty both in the United States and abroad.

Project Mobilize

7674 W. 63rd Street
Summit, IL 60501
email: www.mobilize.org/join-the-movement
website: www.mobilize.org

Project Mobilize is a network of leaders targeting millennials that seeks to create positive change within the system and through existing organizations. It also works to invest in new ideas that would help unify Americans in a progressive manner.

Rock the Vote

1440 G Street NW
Washington, DC 20005
(202) 719-9910
website: www.rockthevote.org

Rock the Vote educates young voters about politics and the election process while encouraging them to become involved at the community level and to vote. The organization has been credited in part for the increased turnout among youth voters in the 2018 midterms.

Young America's Foundation

11480 Commerce Park Drive, Suite 600
Reston, VA 20191-1556
(703) 318-9608
email: https://www.yaf.org/contact-us
website: www.yaf.org

This conservative student group seeks to increase the number of students that are motivated toward ideas of individual freedom, a strong national defense, free enterprise, and traditional values.

Young Democratic Socialists of America

705 Maiden Lane, Suite 702
New York, NY 10038
(917) 830-8416
email: https://y.dsausa.org/contact-us
website: www.mobilize.org/join-the-movement

This political organization works to build the power of students, campus communities, and youth to fight for equality, justice, and democratic socialism.

Bibliography of Books

Best, Joel, and Eric Best. *The Student Loan Mess: How Good Intentions Created a Trillion-Dollar Problem*. Berkeley, CA: University of California Press, 2014.

Frey, William H. *Diversity Explosion: How New Racial Demographics Are Remaking America*. Washington, DC: Brooking Institution Press, 2014.

Gentry, Bobbi. *Why Youth Vote: Identity, Inspirational Leaders, and Independence*. New York, NY: Springer, 2018.

Iceland, John. *A Portrait of America: The Demographic Perspective*. Berkeley, CA: University of California Press, 2014.

Kaufmann, Eric. *White Shift: Populism, Immigration, and the Future of White Majorities*. New York, NY: Harry N. Abrams, 2019.

Mahone, Beverly. *The Baby Boomer Millennial Divide: Making It Work at Work*. Elgin, IL: Document Publishing Group, 2017.

Nowrasteh, Alex. *Open Immigration: Yea and Nay*. New York, NY: Encounter Books, 2014.

Palmer, Anna, and Jake Sherman. *The Hill to Die On: The Battle for Congress and the Future of Trump's America*. New York, NY: Crown Publishing Group, 2019.

Ridout, Travis N. *New Directions in Media and Politics*. London, England: Routledge, 2012.

Schimpff, Stephen C. *The Future of Health-Care Delivery*. Sterling, VA: Potomac Books, 2012.

Shrestha, Laura B. *The Changing Demographic Profile of the United States*. BiblioGov, 2013.

Soltis Anderson, Kristen. *The Selfie Vote: Where Millennials Are Leading America (And How Republicans Can Keep Up)*. Northampton, MA: Broadside Books, 2015.

Spancake, Diane. *Student Loan Forgiveness or Ten Years to Life?* Bloomington, IN: Archway Publishing, 2015.

Spitzer, Robert J. *The Politics of Gun Control*. Boulder, CO: Paradigm Publishers, 2011.

Street, Christopher. *Gun Control: Guns in America, the Full Debate, More Guns Less Problems? No Guns No Problems?* CreateSpace Independent Publishing Platform, 2016.

Index

A

abortion, 16, 126, 179

African Americans, 14, 148, 149, 152–153, 154–155, 156, 184

"all American," 14, 160–161, 164

Amadeo, Kimberly, 107–114

Asian Americans/Asians, 14, 96, 98, 99, 112, 149, 150–153, 156–157, 161, 174, 183, 184

B

baby boomers, aging of, 15, 16, 19, 32, 42, 56–89, 103, 104, 114, 158, 163, 184

not prepared for retirement, 80–84

birth rate, declining, 85–89, 92, 104, 119, 131

border wall, 15, 49, 50, 111

Brownstein, Ron, 159–165

Bush, George W., 100, 109, 153, 155, 164

C

Caumont, Andrea, 182–187

climate change, issue of, 16, 19, 44–48, 88–89, 130–131, 179

Clinton, Bill, 155, 164

Clinton, Hillary, 168

Cohn, D'Vera, 182–187

college

cost of and student debt, 16, 92, 135–145, 185

free tuition, 92, 139–140

conservativism, 15, 16, 19, 40, 56, 148, 164, 168, 169, 173, 179

Cruz, Ted, 171–177

D

Dart, Tom, 171–177

DeAngelis, Tori, 30–37

Democrats, 15, 16, 24, 41, 45, 63, 97, 102, 150–158, 163, 166, 168, 171, 172–177, 178, 180–181

E

Ehrlich, Anne H., 115–121

Ehrlich, Paul, 115–121

electoral future, America's, 148–187

environmental issues, 16, 19, 44–48, 88–89, 115–121, 122–128, 129–134, 179

F

family planning, 45, 125–126, 130, 132

Fottrell, Quentin, 100–101

Frey, William H., 149–158

Friedman, Gerald, 62–68

Furman, Jason, 103–106